HUMANIZING RULES

HUMANIZING RULES

BRINGING BEHAVIOURAL SCIENCE TO ETHICS AND COMPLIANCE

CHRISTIAN HUNT

WILEY

Registered Office(s)

John Wiley & Sons, Inc., 111 River Street, Hoboken, NJ 07030, USA
John Wiley & Sons Ltd, The Atrium, Southern Gate, Chichester, West Sussex, PO19 8SQ, UK

Editorial Office

The Atrium, Southern Gate, Chichester, West Sussex, PO19 8SQ, UK

For details of our global editorial offices, customer services, and more information about Wiley products visit us at www.wiley.com.

Wiley also publishes its books in a variety of electronic formats and by print-on-demand. Some content that appears in standard print versions of this book may not be available in other formats.

Library of Congress Cataloging-in-Publication Data is Available:

ISBN 9781394177400 (Hardback)
ISBN 9781394187287 (ePDF)
ISBN 9781394187294 (ePub)

Cover Design: Wiley
Cover Image: © Misha Shutkevych/Getty Images

SKY10062800_121523

CONTENTS

CONTENTS

PREFACE

What Is This Book About?

Humanizing Rules is a practical guide for anyone whose job involves managing human risk or who is interested in understanding more about it.

What Is Human Risk?

Human risk is "the risk of people doing things they shouldn't, or not doing things they should". It's an intentionally broad definition that covers the full range of risks posed by human decision-making. It includes wilful acts such as "I deliberately set out to commit fraud" and human errors such as "I was tired and made a mistake".

Human risk is the largest risk facing all organisations and society as a whole. When things go wrong, there is always a human component involved. People either cause problems in the first place or make them worse by how they respond.

Who Is the Book For?

Humanizing Rules is designed for anyone responsible for influencing human decision-making to reduce risk or ensure compliance with a set of rules or principles. It can help managers and senior leaders to be more effective in influencing the decisions of their employees and therefore deliver desired business outcomes.

It is also directly relevant to professionals in disciplines such as risk, ethics, legal, and compliance. But it is equally applicable to people in other functions who need to ensure that their fellow employees "comply" with rules, policies, or procedures. This includes but is not limited to functions like audit, legal, human resources, internal comms, procurement, and health & safety. If your role involves mitigating human risk, then *Humanizing Rules* is for you.

The book is written for a lay audience with little or no previous knowledge of either theoretical or practical behavioural science.

What Does It Cover?

Humanizing Rules suggests an approach to managing human decision-making that fuses creativity and behavioural science, the study of the drivers of human decision-making. By bringing behavioural science to "compliance", we can be more effective, mitigate human risk, reduce employee frustration, and get the best out of people.

Traditional approaches to managing human risk typically rely heavily on two presumptions. The first is that employers have the right to tell their employees what to do and that employees will therefore comply. The second is that compliance can be motivated via incentives and noncompliance can be deterred via punishment. These presumptions are theoretically correct, but often fail in practice. If we really want to influence human behaviour, we need to humanize our rules.

The book is designed to be practical. As we explore human behaviour, I will share stories and case studies from various industries and contexts. The ideas and suggestions I share have all been developed in the field. Either when I was working at UBS or in collaboration with my Human Risk clients. All of these ideas and suggestions are presented, not so that you can slavishly copy them – though if you think they might work in your environment, do feel free – but rather to inspire you to come up with your own ideas.

What Doesn't It Cover?

The book is not a step-by-step guide to managing human risk. Nor is it a technical guide to behavioural science or risk management. It is designed to inspire you to think differently about how to approach the challenge and to identify new solutions to old problems.

How Is It Structured?

This book is split into four Parts. Part I begins with a story of a minor error with major consequences that, for reasons I explain, helped to inspire the book. I then explore why we need to humanize rules and how behavioural science can help us to do that. I also explore some basic behavioural science principles and highlight why these are relevant.

Part II introduces HUMANS, a simple, practical framework that will help you to deploy behavioural science techniques in your organisation. If you're introducing something new or refreshing your programme, it'll help you think about how your employees will likely react. If something isn't working as expected, HUMANS can help you diagnose why and improve things. Finally, HUMANS can also help you to predict where other parts of your compliance framework might be under stress and are worthy of your attention.

In Part III, I outline six rules. These aren't rules in a traditional sense of "things you need to follow" but principles that help to highlight common misperceptions about compliance and why they can reduce effectiveness and efficiency in our programmes. The six rules build on HUMANS and are there to help you challenge orthodox thinking and provide some guiding principles to help you think differently about solving compliance challenges.

Part IV will help you to understand where to deploy your newfound knowledge. Using the RADAR framework, we can use the behaviour of our employees to help us identify the biggest disconnects between what we would like them to do and what they are likely to do. These will give you pointers on where to focus your behavioural efforts, so you can target low-hanging fruit, get results quicker, and keep stakeholders on board as you try new things. Finally, I share some thoughts about how you can humanize rules in your organisation. I'll introduce the idea of borrowing from "compliance in the wild" – examples from outside your organisation that you might not immediately think of as relevant – and tell you how to implement the lessons from them.

USER MANUAL

Before we begin, here's a brief user manual for how to get the most out of the book.

How to Use This Book

Since the book is called *Humanizing Rules,* you'll be relieved to hear it isn't a set of rules to be slavishly followed. It contains six specific ones, but don't worry; they're not traditional rules. Like the rest of this book, think of them as you would a travel guide or cookbook. I want to inspire you rather than provide you with an instruction manual to be followed to the letter. *Humanizing Rules* is written with a general audience in mind which should mean that the majority of dynamics I highlight and ideas I suggest are relevant to your situation. But, occasionally, they might not be. If that happens, feel free to adapt the rules to meet your needs, just as you would a travel itinerary or recipe.

Humanizing Rules isn't an academic book that presents the findings of rigorous academic research that has been tested and peer-reviewed. None of the ideas suggested in the book has been tested in laboratory conditions. Most have, however, been tested in the real world, while others are still work in progress. In sharing these, I want to suggest new ideas you might not have previously considered. My hope in doing so is to inspire you to think differently about how you go about things.

Some ideas I propose in the book are counter-intuitive and challenge traditional orthodoxy. There would be little point in writing it if I wasn't going to do that! Sometimes, I will point you towards things that might be challenging to implement, particularly if you are operating in a harsh regulatory environment. My advice is to do what you can. But don't let that be an excuse for not trying new things. Small changes in the right direction are better than no changes. Most importantly, do have fun!

Terminology

As we try to humanize rules, there is a wide range of applications for the ideas I explore. For example, a technique that can help a team leader make it more likely their team will meet a requirement to fill in timesheets can also be used elsewhere. It can help Human Resources departments to encourage managers to attend a training course or by Compliance to get employees to complete a regulatory return.

I have used standard terms throughout the book to avoid confusion and repetition and deliver consistency and simplicity. To avoid misunderstandings, here are the terms I frequently use and an explanation of what they mean:

- *Employees* are the people in your organisation, the primary "target audience" we seek to influence. However, we can also use the same techniques and ideas to persuade other target audiences in entirely different contexts. For example, your customers, suppliers, regulators, investors, or people applying for jobs in your organisation.

- *Rules* are what you want or need your employees to do or not do. What we might call your "desired outcome". The most obvious example of a desired outcome is compliance with the rules you have within your organisation. To avoid being repetitious – and because sometimes I need a different word – I occasionally use "Requirement" instead of "Rule", for example, when I'm referring to the desired outcome of having your employees comply with externally imposed laws or regulations. *Rules* or *Regulations* might also mean following instructions, policies, codes, orders, mandates, or any other instrument or tool used to influence the behaviour of employees. That includes responding in the desired manner to email messages and poster campaigns.

- *Compliance* means the act of complying with something. In other words, doing "what we want them to do" or "what we need them to do". It also captures concepts such as adherence. It is not the same as "big C" Compliance, which I use to refer to the function within an organisation responsible for ensuring compliance with regulations; though, if *compliance* comes at the start of a sentence, then I will capitalise it! Finally, for the avoidance of doubt, the term noncompliance means the opposite of *compliance*.

- *Framework* means the architecture you're using to influence your employees. The most obvious example is a compliance framework, but it can also mean any rules, programmes or systems you're using to deliver your desired outcomes, such as a communications campaign, for example.

- *Asking your employees to do something* means the act of communicating your desired outcome to them. You may prefer to think of it as "telling them what to do", "reminding them of the rules", "giving orders", or "issuing warnings". The verb "ask" isn't intended to suggest that you have no authority over your employees. I use it not only because it is polite but also as a reminder that, often, we need to work with, rather than against, our employees to achieve our desired outcome.

INTRODUCTION

The Wrong Envelope

You Had One Job

Sometimes in life, we say things we later come to regret. Very occasionally, those become "famous last words", something we are likely to regret, if not for the rest of our lives, for a very long time. If we're unlucky, it'll play out in public.

In Brian Cullinan's case, the famous last words were probably something he said in an interview[1] in January 2017:

It doesn't sound very complicated, but you have to make sure you're giving the presenter the right envelope.

Cullinan was talking about his forthcoming role in the 89th Academy of Motion Picture Arts & Sciences Annual Awards. You and I know it as "the Oscars". At the time, Cullinan was a partner at the professional services firm PwC.

The purpose of the – now deleted but very much alive in archive form – interview was to showcase Cullinan and his fellow partner Martha Ruiz's role in supporting the awards.

Unsurprisingly, given the firm they worked for, Cullinan and Ruiz were involved in a simple but crucial logistical exercise. Their job was to count the votes and keep the names of the winners secret until the presenters revealed them during the Oscars ceremony. They would be responsible for handing over red envelopes containing the winner's name to the presenters just before they went on stage. As Cullinan's comment made clear, he had one job to do. In the same interview, he explained that nothing had ever gone wrong.

Hitting the Headlines

Until on 26 February 2017, it did. With most of the ceremony completed without incident, only one award remained. The biggest award of the night; the one for Best Picture. You wouldn't want anything to ever go wrong during the ceremony, but if it were going to happen, this would be the worst possible moment. As you'll already know or have worked out by now, this was the precise moment when Cullinan handed out the wrong envelope, and chaos ensued. If you've never seen it, or haven't watched it for some time, do take a moment to search out a clip on YouTube.

After the ceremony, PwC issued an apologetic statement explaining what had happened:

PwC Partner Brian Cullinan mistakenly handed the back-up envelope for Actress in a Leading Role instead of the envelope for Best Picture to presenters Warren Beatty and Faye Dunaway. Once the error occurred, protocols for correcting it were not followed through quickly enough by Mr Cullinan or his partner.

Thanks to the (in)actions of Cullinan and Ruiz, the winners' names were relegated to being the second biggest story of the night. The Oscars had hit the headlines for all the wrong reasons.

The Business of Influencing Human Decision-Making

As events unfolded in Los Angeles on Sunday night, I was getting ready to start my working week in London. As I waited for my coffee machine to warm up, I mindlessly scrolled through social media. It didn't take long for my feed to fill with video clips from the ceremony. Transfixed, I watched clip after clip, trying to make sense of it. Unbeknownst to the algorithms feeding my insatiable appetite, I wasn't just enjoying the drama. I had a light-bulb moment that would change the course of my career.

At the time, I was a Managing Director at the Swiss Bank UBS, responsible for Compliance and Operational Risk for the firm's asset management division and the EMEA[2] region of the firm as a whole. Compliance, as the name implies, involves ensuring the firm is compliant with all applicable rules and regulations.

Operational or "op" risk is about ensuring the firm minimises and mitigates the impact of "non-financial" threats such as fraud, cyber, or reputational risk. While Financial Services firms make money from taking calculated financial risks, compliance and operational risks are the kinds you want to avoid at all costs.

Having been in post for a few years, I realised that neither my job title nor my responsibilities reflected the substance of my job. Something was missing. But I couldn't work out what. The envelope incident at the Oscars – simultaneously, a compliance breach in not following protocol and an op risk incident – gave me the answer.

Thanks to Brian Cullinan, it suddenly dawned on me that the businesses of compliance and op risk were influencing human decision-making. It wasn't just part of my job. It *was* my job! The only way the firm would be compliant was if we could successfully influence the decision-making of the people within it. After all, you couldn't tell a company to be compliant and expect it to respond! Similar dynamics applied to op risk. Whenever things go wrong – in organisations or society – there is always a human component involved. People can create problems, for example, by giving out the wrong envelope at an awards ceremony. They can also make them worse by how they respond. Or, in the case of an awards ceremony where the wrong envelope has been handed out, don't respond.

While I didn't expect ever to have to deal with the risks associated with the delivery of award envelopes at a globally televised awards ceremony – though, as ever with risk, never say never – the case of the wrong envelope taught me a valuable lesson. Properly understanding human decision-making was a vital skill I would need to master. People, it seemed to me, were the most significant driver of risk facing the organisation, and it was my job to help mitigate that.

The Riskiest Part of Banking Isn't the Banking

I wasn't the only person thinking in those terms. Later that year, in an interview with *Bloomberg Markets* magazine, my ultimate boss, the then CEO of UBS, Sergio Ermotti, said:

> The riskiest part of our business nowadays is operational risks. We can have hours of discussion on credit or market risks. But the one thing that really hurt in the last ten years of our industry is op risks, not credit or market risks. If you do something wrong as a bank, or you have people doing bad things within the bank, it costs you much more than any credit risk or market position.[3]

3

Which, when you think about it, is quite a statement! He was essentially saying that the riskiest thing about banking isn't the banking. The riskiest thing, Ermotti is saying, is poor decision-making by the bank or its employees. Notice how he distinguishes between doing "something wrong as a bank" and "people doing bad things within the bank". You can see something similar in PwC's statement about the Oscars incident. By emphasising a failure to follow protocol, they're seeking to reinforce the fact the organisation didn't sanction the "bad" behaviour.

To understand why Ermotti might choose to differentiate between the firm's and its employees' decisions, we need to go back to the circumstances of his appointment. In 2011, he'd become CEO of UBS following the resignation of his predecessor Ossie Grubel after the discovery of a rogue trader in the firm's investment bank. Between 2008 and 2011, a trader called Kweku Adoboli engaged in unauthorised trading activities that ultimately resulted in $2.3 billion in losses. At one point in time, Adoboli's trading positions exposed the firm to risk of losses of an eye-watering $11.8 billion.

It's a story I know well because it unfolded on my watch. On September 14, 2011, Adoboli, already subject to a UBS internal investigation into his trading activities, left the office and sent an email admitting what he'd done.

Just ten days earlier, I'd started a new job at the Financial Services Authority, the industry's then regulator, as the head of department responsible for supervising the UK operations of non-UK banks. Since Adoboli was based in London, it fell to my team to lead the regulatory response. As we investigated what had happened, our work focused on understanding how Adoboli had managed to do what he did and ensuring there couldn't be a repeat. But on a personal level, we couldn't help wondering what had driven him and how he'd justified his actions to himself.

Many of the answers came during Adoboli's trial. I was particularly struck by the words of the judge who, in sentencing him to seven years in prison, told him he was

---

profoundly unselfconscious of your own failings. There is the strong streak of the gambler in you, born out by your personal trading. You were arrogant enough to think that the bank's rules for traders did not apply to you. And you denied that you were a rogue trader, claiming that at all times you were acting in the bank's interests, while conveniently ignoring that the real characteristic of the rogue trader is that he ignores the rules designed to manage risk.[4]

4

We often think of bad outcomes as caused by actions; for example, people "taking a risk", "making mistakes" or "committing crimes". But inaction can be equally, if not more, dangerous if the thing they're not doing is critical. Forgetting to lock a door, failing to stop at a red light or ignoring evidence of wrongdoing are all things that can lead to bad outcomes.

The definition also includes a word I am often asked about; "things". It is, people tell me, a surprisingly "loose" word to include in a definition; that's deliberate. When people used to ask me what "operational risk" was about, I'd tell them it involved "trying to stop bad things from happening". That usually elicited a follow-up statement, posing as a question: "why are you only trying to stop them? Shouldn't you actually be stopping them?". My response was that if I knew what they were, of course, I'd stop them. Obviously, I didn't. That's why the word "things" is there.

One of the challenges of risk is that we can't always predict exactly what might go wrong. But we know that whatever it is, it will involve humans. We also know that whenever something goes wrong in organisations, someone somewhere knew something, that could have helped to prevent it.

In this book, I'm going to help you think about how to humanize rules to mitigate human risk. I'm also going to help you promote human reward.

Human Reward

If human beings pose so much risk, then why do we employ them? The answer is pretty obvious; we need to! Ask any CEO of a successful company what their biggest asset is, and chances are they'll tell you it's their people. The reason organisations spend vast amounts on paying people is because they are seen as a competitive advantage.

That has always been true, though the role they fulfil has changed and is changing. Historically, people were providers of manual labour. Nowadays, the ease with which companies in all sectors can deploy machines that are better and more cost-effective than humans at both physical and computational tasks means the role people play within organisations is rapidly shifting. We're hiring people to do things the machines can't. At least, not yet. Tasks that involve skills like emotional intelligence, creativity, and judgement. This is when we are at our best. But it is also when we are at our riskiest.

The challenge facing organisations is, therefore, a balancing act between mitigating human risk and what I call "human reward" – getting the best out of them. Note "best" not "most"– this isn't about exploiting people. Human risk and human reward are interrelated. If you over-emphasise human risk, you'll miss opportunities for human reward. If you over-emphasise human reward – by, for example, saying to your employees, "do whatever it takes to hit your sales target" – you'll run unnecessary human risk. That's the balancing act facing companies in the twenty-first century.

In *Humanizing Rules*, I will explore how we can manage the tension between those two dynamics. If we hire people because they're smart, then it's probably not a good idea to treat them in a manner that suggests we think the opposite. But equally, as we've seen from Cullinan and Adoboli, intelligent people don't always make wise decisions.

This book isn't about preventing outliers, like the next Kweku Adoboli. For that, we'll need to review incentive frameworks, monitoring and surveillance programmes and disciplinary processes. Instead, it looks at the day-to-day processes that we deploy to influence every employee; the controls, the processes, the frameworks, the communications campaigns, the training, and, above all, the rules. By humanizing those, we can get the best out of our people, while mitigating risk.

We'll begin our journey by looking at perspective. If we want to influence our employees effectively, we need to think less about things from our perspective and more from theirs.

Notes

1. The original article has now been deleted, but you can read it via the Wayback Machine here: https://web.archive.org/web/20170213234409/https://medium.com/art-science/what-it-feels-like-to-count-oscar-votes-f89a38efdf1c

2. EMEA is Europe, the Middle East, and Africa. At UBS, this does not include the home market of Switzerland, which is classified as a separate region.

3. https://humanizingrules.link/adoboli

4. https://www.judiciary.uk/wp-content/uploads/JCO/Documents/Judgments/kweku-adoboli-sentencing-remarks-20112012.pdf

5. At the time of writing this book, that "title" is held by Jérôme Kerviel, whose $6.9 billion losses at French bank Société Générale between 2006 and 2008 dwarfed Adoboli's more modest $2.3 billion.

PART I
INTRODUCING BEHAVIOURAL SCIENCE

CHAPTER 1
A MATTER
OF PERSPECTIVE

Gone Fishing

In a short story called "An anecdote on the lowering of productivity at work",[1] German author Heinrich Böll tells the story of a tourist who comes across a fisherman sitting idly on his boat. The tourist asks the fisherman why he's not out fishing. The fisherman explains that he's already caught enough fish for two days. Unsolicited, the tourist offers his opinion, telling the fisherman that if he worked harder, he could build up a fishing empire. The fisherman asks him what would happen then. The tourist tells him he will be able to retire and relax on his boat. "But," says the fisherman, "I'm already doing that!" The tourist walks away, reflecting on how he used to think that the reason he worked was to one day not have to work.

Though it wasn't Böll's motivation for writing the story,[2] it's a good illustration of the power of perception. Two people can look at the same situation and draw entirely different conclusions. From the tourist's perspective, the fisherman is lazy and unproductive. From the fisherman's perspective, his lifestyle suits him perfectly. By the end, the tourist starts seeing things as the fisherman does.

In this book, I'm going to help *you* become the tourist. Not to observe a fisherman who prioritises his work-life balance but to obtain insights into what your employees think about the rules that you are asking them to comply with. By obtaining those insights, we'll be able to find ways of asking them, which are more likely to succeed. If you're thinking, "Can't we just tell them what to do?", I'll address that shortly. To do so, let me introduce you to the "Employment Contract Fallacy".

The Employment Contract Fallacy

If you're a senior manager or the owner of a business, I'm going to let you into a little secret you might not want to hear: the average employee in your company doesn't care about your company. At least, not as much as you do. What they primarily care about are the things that matter to them; such as "Is my job secure?", "Do I feel valued?", and "Do I get on with my work colleagues?"

If you can help to meet those concerns, then your employees are more likely to care about the company because the company cares about them. Yet, while significant efforts are often made to align those interests when it comes to remuneration and lifestyle benefits, there is often far less effort put into another area: compliance.

Where compliance is concerned, something I call the "Employment Contract Fallacy" can often kick in. It presumes that because an employment contract exists between the company and the employee, the employer can tell the employee what to do and expect compliance. From a legal perspective, of course, they can. But that doesn't necessarily give them the moral authority to do so; and, as we'll come on to see, that can be critical in specific contexts.

We all know that, in reality, just because someone has signed a contract doesn't mean they subjugate all of their personal priorities to the other party. When I rent a car, I don't automatically prioritise the interests of the car rental company above my own. Nor does the rental company suddenly prioritise my interests above its own.

Think about the awful process we go through to pick up a car and check it back in. Usually, it involves being made to wait a long time before being required to provide multiple signatures to agree to things we aren't given time to read. We intuitively know that what we're being asked to sign is more in the rental company's interests than our own. Then, when checking the car back in, we know – unless we've bought the usuriously priced insurance excess waiver – that the rental firm will inspect the vehicle looking for the most minor of scratches. The rental agreement overshadows every aspect of that relationship, making it feel very transactional.

Attestation

No company wants a relationship with its employees akin to the kind induced by the average car rental agreement. Yet many use processes that replicate precisely this dynamic. For example, the annual attestation process that requires employees to confirm something along the lines of the fact that they have read, understood, memorised, and are compliant with all of the company's rules and policies. On the face of it, this is a sensible way for organisations to ensure that their employees comply. After all, they're reminding them of their obligations and asking for confirmation that they're aware of and complying with them.

But if we think about it from the employee's perspective, the situation looks somewhat different. They don't really have a choice but to sign the attestation to keep their job. There is usually no opportunity to say, "Actually, I don't understand this policy" or "Come to think of it, I haven't complied with that rule". The form might seem reasonable, but the substance often feels very unreasonable. They're being asked to sign something that reminds them of a car rental agreement, but where the stakes are far higher!

It is not implausible that a sizeable proportion of employees, when faced with the attestation they're required to make, will just blindly sign to tick the box; a box, that is, that they know is entirely in the company's interests and not their own.

There is a further downside to this approach. It can suggest to the employee that the company prioritises box-ticking over substance. After all, if they really wanted their employees to read, understand, memorise, and be compliant with that many policies, they would make them significantly shorter and easier to read. When the "substance" is at odds with the "form", we'll look at substance every time.

Induction Training

Induction training provides another illustration of this dynamic. Like car rental companies, most employers are usually very good at marketing before people sign the contract and less good at some aspects of the actual experience. The effort made when recruiting staff is often neglected at the point when the employee joins.

One of the best examples of this disconnect is induction training, particularly in larger organisations where "sheep dip" processes occur weekly.

When employees join a new organisation, their immediate focus is on logistical questions, like "Where are the toilets?" and "How do I buy food in the canteen?". They'll also have more emotional questions such as "What are my colleagues like?" and "Have I made the right decision to join this company?".

Yet the content they are presented with during induction training often focuses on entirely different issues. Companies frequently see it as an opportunity to download information into new employees' brains so they can tick the box to say it's been done. Topics like risk and compliance frameworks are presented alongside marketing messages about how great the company is. Often they show a video featuring a disembodied voice saying things like, "Welcome to MegaCorp. With over 5,000 offices, we're one of the oldest and biggest...". Typically, the CEO then makes a cameo appearance via video to talk about values and how ethics and compliance are really important.

It's well-intentioned. But no one in the audience is wondering what the risk framework looks like! Nor do they need to be told how many offices the company has. After all, they've applied for a job there, so chances are they already know. They don't need a sales pitch about the company since they've already decided to join it. What they need is reassurance they've made the right decision. As for the CEO's "say the right thing" speech, there's the risk of an unintended subliminal message. Why, the audience may wonder, are they talking about ethics? If it were genuinely an ethical company, there would be no need to say it because it would be evident from how people behaved.

I'm not suggesting that the agenda should be entirely driven by what the employees want. There will be some things the company needs to communicate that need to be said at that point. But all too often, the agenda is filled with things that the new employees aren't receptive to hearing because they're focussed on other priorities. Boxes are ticked from the company's perspective, but the new employees might not have received the message.

Induction training doesn't end when people leave that room. In fact, the most compelling part of it might well begin at precisely that point. Because that is when the theory ends and the practice starts. It's when the new employees get to see what really happens on the ground. You can tell people it's an ethical company, but if they see that the reality is entirely different, they will take their lead from that and not the training. Therefore, it might be worth investing more effort in planning their first contact with reality than the stylised training session that greets them on arrival.

Because We Employ You, We Can Tell You What to Do

From a legal perspective, the Employment Contract Fallacy is, of course, not a fallacy. An employment contract *does* give employers the right to impose specific requirements on employees. They can, for example, instruct their employees where to work, what times they need them to be at work and, in many cases, what to wear. Using these legal rights is appropriate in some environments, notably in safety-critical industries. It is, by any measure, entirely reasonable for a nuclear power station operator to require its employees to follow strict protocols. We wouldn't want people working in the power station to have the freedom to "see what would happen" if they altered the mix in the reactor just because they felt like it!

In those cases, the interests of the employer and the employee *are* naturally aligned. An aircrew has the same interest in ensuring the plane they are flying makes it safely to its destination as the airline employing them. But there may be decisions the airline takes in the interests of collective safety that aren't in the interests of the individual members of the aircrew. Perhaps it determines that having staff flying the same route all the time is better for safety since they will be familiar with it. That isn't in the interests of an aircrew that enjoys the experience of flying to different destinations and having variety at work. It might be in the airline's best interests to cut staff wages or change working terms and conditions to ensure it meets cost or profitability targets. But it isn't in the interests of the air-crew. In those cases, the interests of the two are far less aligned. Unless, of course, the company is in really dire straits and the cuts are to ensure survival.

There are lots of things that employers have the legal right to demand from their employees – either as a matter of law or under a specific employment contract – that employees might not find acceptable. An employer could, for example, decide that the reputational risk posed by employees having personal social media accounts is outside their risk appetite and so seek to ban them from doing so. Even if it's entirely within the organisation's legal rights to do so, many employees might see it as a case of employer "over-reach". Of course, much would depend on the nature of the employer. Those working for a national security service, for whom a social media account might present a personal risk, are more willing to accept it than those working for a typical company.

Contracts Are for Disputes, Not Relationships

As anyone involved in a contractual dispute can attest, the moment we're using contractual terms to justify or enforce a particular outcome, it means something has gone wrong! If you have to rely on the fact that your employee has signed a contract to justify telling them what to do, you've shifted the terms of the relationship from mutual trust and cooperation to one ruled by contract.

The Employment Contract Fallacy means we often think of getting our employees to behave in a particular manner as a communications challenge, not an engagement exercise. That is a huge mistake. This brings me to, by far, the most critical lesson of the entire book:

> To be effective at influencing our employees' behaviour means we need to focus not on what we would *like* them to do but on what they are *likely to do*.

In other words, we need to get past the Employment Contract Fallacy and recognise that we can't always rely on just telling them what to do.

What's In It for Me?

In this chapter, we've primarily focussed on things from the employee's perspective. In part, I'm trying to challenge conventional wisdom, which tends to see things from the employer's perspective; the "you're lucky to have a job here" logic. But also because the time and money we invest in people demand that we get the best out of them. Our employee's attention span and cognitive abilities are all scarce resources that we need to treat as such. We're more likely to do that if we think about things from their perspective.

As we'll see in later chapters, it is also entirely in the employer's interest to think in these terms. Regardless of which industry you're in, there will be times when you need to ask people to do things that will make life more difficult for them. There will also be times when we can't monitor what they are doing, and we'll only find out things have gone wrong after the event. And there will be tasks with a qualitative component where we need our employees to be engaged to achieve our desired outcome.

Humanizing rules doesn't mean we just let our employees have their way. We shouldn't scrap rules or change what we ask of our employees simply because what we require will prove unpopular. Just as we wouldn't give in to every whim of a disgruntled teenager, we shouldn't always do what our employees want. For good reason, requirements often make life harder for all of us. Sometimes an outcome that is good societally or for a group of people requires individuals to make sacrifices.

Unlike the traditional adage about the customer always being right, the employee isn't. But we should make an effort to understand how what we're asking them to do is likely to come across. That way, we'll know when we're asking a lot of them and when we're not. If we learn that "what we would like them to do" is close to "what they are likely to do", we can expend less effort on that particular requirement than when the two are far apart. This means that we'll be able to identify opportunities where we can push them further than we might otherwise, as well as opportunities where we might choose to row back.

New Perspective, New Job

Understanding things from our employee's perspective isn't just about a shift in attitude. It also means we need to think less about the objective we're trying to deliver and more about the techniques that will get us there. There is often a big difference between a corporate objective and the realities of what that means on the ground. To deliver the former, we need to understand that the task facing us is the latter. In the next chapters, we'll look at how we can identify the right tools for that job.

Notes

1. The story has been widely translated into English. I recommend this version: https://humanizingrules.link/fish

2. As a political writer, Böll's focus in the story is much more about critiquing capitalism.

CHAPTER 2
RIGHT TOOLS
FOR THE JOB

Scissors, But for Pizza

I'm a big fan of kitchen gadgets. While many of those I've bought sit unloved at the bottom of a drawer, there's one that gets regular use: the pizza scissors. I got mine to replace one of those wheel-shaped cutters that promise much but deliver nothing but disappointment. If you're unfamiliar with the concept of pizza scissors, imagine an exaggerated version of a regular pair of scissors. There's an angled handle that prevents scalding from steaming hot pizza. Not to mention the extra-long blades that slice whatever pizza you've got, deep dough or crunchy crust, perfectly every time. Trust me on this; when it comes to cutting pizza, they're just what you need.

Pizza scissors are an excellent example of something my father refers to as "the right tool for the job". As he explained to me time and time again when I was growing up – though he definitely wasn't talking about pizza scissors – we're more likely to be able to complete tasks safely and efficiently if we're using equipment that is specifically designed for that purpose. You can cut pizza using regular scissors, but you'll get a much better result using pizza scissors. You'll also have a lot more fun.

The Right Tools for the Job

Having the right tool for the job is also essential when asking our employees to follow our rules. Unlike cutting pizza – where the solution is now apparent to you! – this poses a far greater set of challenges.

The first relates to the importance of perspective that I explored in Chapter 1. If we want to select the right tools for the job, we need to define the job from our employees' perspectives and not our own. We need to think less about their theoretical understanding of a particular task or how we would *like* them to feel about it and more about the realities of what they actually know and how they truly feel.

The second is that our employees are sentient, unlike the pizza, which does not know it is being cut. The tools we choose have a signalling effect. As we'll see, many techniques we commonly deploy often don't consider things from the employee's perspective. As a result, they often antagonise, irritate, or send unhelpful signals to the very people we're trying to influence.

The third is that when selecting our tools, we can unnecessarily limit ourselves to a traditional toolkit, which may not be suitable. As a result, we define the problem by reference to the tools we have rather than the ones we should or could have. The proverb: "If all you have is a hammer, then everything looks like a nail", comes to mind. To put it another way, we don't think to buy pizza scissors, so we persist in using our prehistoric wheel.

To illustrate how challenging these dynamics are, in Chapter 3, I'm going to open the traditional toolkit. When we look at the tools we find, we can see they're not always as effective as we might think.

CHAPTER 3
THE TRADITIONAL TOOLKIT

What We've Always Done

If there's one answer to a question that always leaves me baffled, it's this: "That's the way we do things around here." I tend to get it when asking for an explanation of a process that makes absolutely no sense to me. As non-explanations go, it's right up there with "because I said so".

Usually, when I get that answer, it's a sign that the person I'm asking either doesn't know or doesn't care. I'm not sure which is worse. What intrigues me is that I hear it far more often than I would expect. I commonly hear it when I'm looking at something I call the "traditional toolkit", i.e., the "tried and tested" techniques often deployed to deliver compliance outcomes.

It's that toolkit that I want to explore in this chapter. Because if ever there was a "way we do things around here" that we should be questioning, then it's that.

Back to Childhood

I want to unpack the toolkit to highlight some of the reasons why these tools can often be ineffective or counter-productive. Not because the tools are inherently wrong but because we're often deploying them without thinking about how effective they might be.

The simplest way I have found to explore the components of the traditional toolkit is to reference an experience we've all had: childhood. Many techniques we use to influence adults in a work environment are ones we experienced as children. Which means you should recognise them. Either because you remember them being used on you or – if you have children – because you're now using them yourself!

In the following sections, I will explore four techniques often used to influence employees:

1. Orders
2. Rules & Principles
3. Bribery & Punishment
4. The Marketing Approach.

In exploring these techniques, I'll trace our steps from early childhood to our teenage years and highlight in broad terms why a particular approach is adopted. Then we'll look at examples of the technique used "in the wild" where road safety provides some interesting illustrations of how these work in practice.

For obvious reasons, what I will describe is intentionally an oversimplification. The idea isn't to provide an academic analysis of these techniques. Instead, it's to inspire you to think about whether the methods that you are deploying in your organisation are as effective as they could be.

Orders

The first tool is something I call "Orders". When we first arrive on this planet, we find ourselves in a heavily controlled environment. Decisions are made on our behalf, and we are expected to follow orders. Every move that we make as a toddler is carefully controlled. To the extent that we are given any autonomy, it is within tightly controlled parameters.

There is an understandable logic to this draconian regime. We have absolutely no experience of the world we inhabit, display natural tendencies to go on voyages of discovery, and are incredibly vulnerable. Given that recipe for disaster, it's not surprising our parents want to control every aspect of our existence.

Orders in the Wild

The most common places where we find "Orders" being used "in the wild" are in safety-critical environments; the kind of workplace where failure to follow the rules to the letter could be a matter of life and death. This makes a lot of sense.

After all, we wouldn't want the people who maintain aircraft to bring a sense of creativity to their work by seeing what happens if they screw the wheels on the wrong way. Nor do we want someone working in a restaurant kitchen to decide that they don't like the existing hygiene protocols and that they will now dry their hands by wiping them with raw chicken. In those environments, most employees will understand why orders are being given. But if we deploy them in environments where people are hired to be creative or innovative, we're likely to face resistance.

We can see sensible applications of it in a road safety context. Take the humble "Stop" sign. This is deployed in situations where, regardless of road conditions, time of day or vehicle being driven, it makes sense to require all drivers to come to a halt. There are virtually no situations in which that instruction would be detrimental to road safety. For an even more draconian sign, consider "No Entry". Unlike "Stop", there's absolutely no sense of agency here. It's something that drivers must comply with under all circumstances.

As we can see from these examples, Orders work well in a predictable environment, where the likelihood of unintended consequences is therefore limited. In the world of aircraft maintenance, the laws of physics will apply consistently. Food hygiene, based on the laws of chemistry, also lends itself to binary rules.

Orders are also effective if we can clearly define what we need people to do or not do. They become less appropriate if any flexibility, nuance, or judgement is required. My rule of thumb is that if you can write a checklist, then orders probably makes sense. Perfect for toilet cleaning instructions, less so for a concierge in a five-star hotel.

Rules & Principles

The second tool is something I call "Rules & Principles". As we get older and gain more world experience, the level of trust that our parents feel able to show in us increases. Rather than just being told what to do, we are allowed greater freedom within predefined constraints.

These constraints can come in the form of rules like "you must be home before seven" or "no internet access until you've finished your homework". Alternatively, they might be broader principles like "be kind to your siblings" – where what is "kind" is left open to interpretation – or "remember not to talk to any strangers".

Rules & Principles in the Wild

Whereas Orders tend to be restricted to specific environments, "Rules & Principles" are prolific and found everywhere.

In simple terms, we can think of Rules working well where we have a specific desired outcome that can easily be codified. On the other hand, Principles can help where a more general outcome is required and writing a rule would be difficult, or it would be open to abuse. Rules can often be bent, but Principles generally can't.

A good example of Rules & Principles "in the wild" is the UK Highway Code.[1] This user-friendly guide is designed to give road users a basic understanding of the Rules that apply to them. It's primarily read by new drivers who are examined on the contents as part of their driving test, but in theory, all drivers are supposed to consult it regularly. The Code combines both Rules and Principles.

The Rules come in the form of legal requirements, which is a criminal offence not to comply with. These are described in the Code as things you either "MUST" or "MUST NOT" do. For example, you MUST stop at a STOP sign and you MUST NOT drive through a red traffic light.

The Principles, which are called "advisory rules" – so, yes, I am stretching things a little here – have no legal force, but can be used in evidence if someone is taken to court for a traffic offence. These use advisory wording such as "should", "should not", "do" or "do not".

Another UK Code, the Takeover Code,[2] is an even better illustration of how Principles and Rules can work together. This Code consists of 6 general Principles and 38 Rules. While the Principles are general in nature and must, therefore, always be adhered to, the Rules are more specific. They can be disapplied if their application is deemed inappropriate or contrary to the spirit of the Principles. For example, a Principle in the Code is that all shareholders must be treated equally. If the application of a particular Rule were to inadvertently result in an outcome that did not deliver that Principle, then it can–with the consent of the Takeover Panel which regulates activity governed by the Code – be overridden.

Bribery & Punishment

The third tool is "Bribery & Punishment". As teenagers, if not before, we become acquainted with the power of economic incentives. Outcomes previously delivered via Rules & Principles or Orders are now subject to market forces.

By way of a simple example, if our parents want us to tidy our bedroom, they can use pocket money as a lever. Their first option is to use Bribery – more politely, a "rewards-based" approach – by saying, "If you tidy your room, you will get some additional pocket money." The second is to deploy Punishment by saying, "I'm not giving you your pocket money because you haven't tidied your room."

In both cases, pocket money is being used as a tool to incentivise the desired outcome. The difference between the two approaches is that the bribe offers additional money, whereas the punishment withholds previously earned money.

As an aside, I also recall similar techniques being deployed by my grandmother. She used them to encourage my grandfather to refrain from monopolising the conversation at the dinner table. Then, the incentive wasn't pocket money, it was dessert!

Bribery & Punishment in the Wild

Bribery & Punishment rely on three key presumptions:

1. People need to be incentivised or disincentivised from undertaking a particular course of action. In other words, they won't do what we need or want of their own accord, so additional measures are required.

2. The activity that is subject to the approach is capable of being monitored. If there is a qualitative component – for example, "tidy your bedroom properly" – the monitoring needs to be able to track that aspect of it.

3. It is appropriate and feasible to use Bribery & Punishment. It may be that the activity does not lend itself to this or that it sets an undesirable precedent. If, for example, we treat ethics or compliance as something that

requires incentives or punishment, then we risk sending a signal that it's an outcome we wouldn't normally expect; hence we have to force it.

As readers who are parents will know, once you turn something into a financial transaction, it is almost impossible to turn it back into a voluntary one. The same applies to adults, by the way. If you want to see how introducing financial incentives can be entirely inappropriate, don't take a bottle of wine the next time you're invited to dinner at a friend's house. Just ask for the bill at the end!

The most obvious example of Punishment – besides jail, but that felt a little extreme – is in a road safety context, where speed cameras deter people from driving above the speed limit. Then there are the various points systems designed to deter drivers from breaking motoring laws. Interestingly, there are multiple approaches to solving the identical problem. In the UK, drivers start with zero points on their licence and have them added for misdemeanours up to 12 points. In Australia, drivers also begin with zero but have demerit points subtracted for offences, with the lowest possible score of minus 13. Meanwhile, in Italy, drivers start with 20 points, receive two points for every two years of clean driving up to a maximum of 30 and lose points if they commit a misdemeanour!

It is somewhat harder to find examples of where we financially reward good behaviour in a motoring context! However, an experiment in 2010 in Stockholm came close. On a stretch of road where breaking the speed limit was common, drivers whose speeding was captured by the speed cameras would be fined. The proceeds of the fines were used as a prize for a lottery. Owners of vehicles driving within the speed limit were automatically entered into it.

More common is an approach adopted by insurers who put "black box" telematic recorders into people's vehicles to monitor their driving and, therefore, what risk they pose from an insurance perspective. Drivers deemed to be "safer" from an insurance perspective are offered discounts on their insurance, a form of financial incentive.

The Marketing Approach

As we become young adults, we expect greater autonomy and are less likely to respond well to other dynamics. At this point, our parents turn to what I call the Marketing Approach. We're given more freedom but must listen to lectures about the risks we might not have considered. They then hope that we've been paying attention.

Sometimes this can be very effective. When I was a teenager, my parents – who are nonsmokers but at the time had cigarettes available for use by visitors who smoked – tried what I thought was a bold strategy. They pointed out where I could find cigarettes in the house and told me I could help myself and no questions would be asked. However, I was also given clear instructions on how to smoke "properly". In particular, they highlighted the need to inhale deeply to "fully enjoy" the experience. Needless to say, I did not!

The Marketing Approach in the Wild

Marketing works well where we can't or don't want to enforce hard rules. It relies on the presumption that the people whose behaviour we're trying to control can be trusted to do the right thing. Or that we recognise that we cannot control what they are doing and are forced to rely on persuasion without a tougher alternative. The presumption or hope is that they will do the right thing if we make them aware of risks that might not be obvious.

The most obvious recent application of Marketing has been during the COVID pandemic, where governments have used it to encourage the population to follow guidelines that are difficult to enforce or codify in rules. It's something we'll explore in more detail in a later chapter.

In a road safety context, we can see this in Safety Awareness campaigns, where the authorities recognise that there are behaviours they can't control but want to avoid. There is, for example, a risk when people drive while tired. However, this is very hard to regulate since you can't set limits in the way you can for alcohol. Even if you could, measuring how much sleep people have had is impossible, so you can't monitor compliance. It would also not be a credible threat. Pointing out the dangers of falling asleep at the wheel is likely to be far more effective than other methods.

Blunt Instruments

Now that we've briefly explored four of the most common traditional compliance tools, what can we learn from them? The first thing to be aware of is that there is nothing inherently wrong with any of these tools. They all have their uses.

After all, there's a reason I can provide examples of each one being deployed. They clearly do work in certain circumstances. But that doesn't mean that they'll work in all cases.

However, these tools are incredibly blunt instruments that rely on presumptions about human behaviour that, as we will see, are not always valid. While we might take comfort from the fact that we recognise them from our childhood, there are reasons why what might work in a family environment is not something we should be copying.

A poor choice of tool can more easily be rectified in a family environment. In part because parents can intuitively flex their approach to meet the moment's needs. The nature of the relationship between the "rule-setters" and the "rule-following" in a family situation is also intended to be a lifelong one. In most cases, this means a baseline level of trust and mutual respect that can smooth out any problems.

There is also a natural balance in play since the rule-setting parent, who initially holds all the power, instinctively knows that one day the "rule-following" child will be able to do things they can no longer control. This means it is far easier for parents to recover from a poor choice of tool than an employer.

Escalation Risk

The risk with deploying these types of tools is that we assume they are effective because they are familiar. If other companies in our sector adopt a similar approach, it can be tempting to adopt the same "best practice" they have. Yet "tried and tested" can often actually be "tried and failed"; we know from experience that the tools often don't work the way we might hope. When that happens, we can easily find ourselves adopting one of two different approaches:

The first is to throw more tools at the problem. If one technique hasn't worked, we double down and use more of it. This leads to logic such as "we gave them training, so the reason we had breaches of our rule must be because we didn't do enough training", without thinking about whether there might be too much training!

The second is to assume that the problem is that we've given our employees too much autonomy. If Marketing hasn't worked, we need to move back to Rules. If Rules haven't worked, we need to move back to Orders. This makes perfect logical sense, but it ignores that the people we're influencing will notice this and react accordingly. They're unlikely to respond well.

Just as we can't easily remove financial incentives for a particular activity once we've introduced them, it is hard to move back from a draconian position once we're there. If you've shifted back to Orders because Rules didn't work, you can't easily go back the other way.

The Behavioural Toolkit

For these reasons, we need to think about broadening our toolkit so that we have some alternatives. Of course, we should continue to use the existing tools where they work. To know when that's the case, we need to understand the behavioural dynamics that underpin them. Where we recognise that they aren't actually working – or that they come with unintended consequences that outweigh the reason for introducing them – we need alternatives.

It's why I'm a proponent of the Behavioural Toolkit: one that uses tools designed to understand how humans actually make decisions rather than how we'd *like* them to take decisions. Not only will that deliver better results, but we'll also have an idea of when things don't work as planned and why that might be. We can then refine our approach. In later chapters, we'll explore some key drivers of human decision-making. By understanding those, we can start thinking about designing more effective tools.

Before we do that, I want to return to the question of what the "job" is that we need the tools for. By looking at two simple examples in Chapter 4, we can see how not all outcomes are identical. As a result, we might need different tools.

Notes

1. The Highway Code is published by the UK Department for Transport and can be viewed here: https://humanizingrules.link/code

2. As the name implies, the Takeover Code governs takeover-related activity and is primarily designed to ensure fair treatment for all shareholders and an orderly framework for takeover bids. It can be viewed here: https://humanizingrules.link/takeover

CHAPTER 4
WHAT *IS* THE JOB?

There Are Rules, and There Are Rules

We often think of all compliance outcomes as the same; rules, you might say, are rules. Yet, in reality, what we are trying to achieve in one situation can often be very different to another. Sometimes, we'll need people to complete a task to a particular standard. In others, we'll need them to do something, even when no one is watching. It would be more apt to say that there are rules, and there are rules!

In this chapter, I will illustrate that when we think about the "job" we're trying to do, that can mean very different things. First, by looking at two things governments asked us all to do during the COVID pandemic. On the face of it, they're both compliance requirements. Yet, when we look at the detail, there are enormous differences. Second, by looking in more detail at training. It's something we use as a catch-all tool, yet the outcomes we need and it can deliver, can be broad. Or, to put it another way, there is training, and there is training.

COVID Compliance

The COVID pandemic has been the world's largest-ever compliance experiment. For the first item ever, virtually everyone on the planet was asked to comply with new sets of rules. It was also the world's largest behavioural science experiment. Not just how people responded to governments but also how governments responded to the pandemic itself.

For academics like Professor Yuval Feldman, who specialises in behavioural law – the intersection between law and behavioural science – and is the author of the highly recommended book, *The Law of Good People*,[1] COVID proved to be, and at the time of writing continues to be, a unique opportunity for field studies.

On a recent episode of my Human Risk podcast, he highlighted the difference between two things that most governments asked their population to do. The first was to wear a mask. The second was to get vaccinated. Both desired outcomes required the population to take action. Yet that's where the similarities end because they are very different in terms of what they need people to do.

In very simple terms, for someone to be able to wear a mask requires them (1) to understand how to wear a mask properly; (2) to have a mask available; (3) to be in environments where they feel comfortable doing so; and (4) motivated to do so on an ongoing basis.

By contrast, in equally simple terms, for someone to be vaccinated simply requires them (1) to know how to book a vaccine appointment; (2) to be able to get to a vaccine centre for that appointment at the right date and time; and (3) to feel motivated enough to attend.

You'll immediately notice from this comparison that mask-wearing is an ongoing "burden" for the individual. At the same time, vaccination is a series of one-off events where professional help is available. Compliance with mask-wearing has a qualitative component; you need to wear your mask correctly to be effective. On the other hand, vaccines are administered by medical professionals; you just need to turn up and roll up your sleeve.

The techniques that are effective in persuading people to wear masks are different from those that are effective in persuading people to be vaccinated.

In Chapter 19, we'll explore whether 100% compliance is something we should strive for. Spoiler alert: it isn't. Thanks to herd immunity, from a virology perspective, we don't need every single person to wear a mask or have a vaccine to stop the spread of the virus. But we do need the vast majority to do so.

We also don't need everyone to wear their masks perfectly. In fact, for reasons we'll explore in the following few chapters, we might arguably be better off having some people wear masks badly rather than not wearing them at all. But not everyone.

Training or Box-Ticking?

If you've ever worked in a big company, you'll almost certainly have experienced the joys of mandatory e-learning. Very often, those courses use a very predictable format:

- Give the training a very dull title that seems utterly irrelevant and open with a very uninspiring introduction.

- Then use a combination of stock images, a dull voiceover and "slow reveal" bullet point-led slides to deliver the content.

- Ensure participants have to click every so often to check they're still awake and ask performative quiz questions throughout to check the "knowledge" they've gleaned.

- Finally, award the participant a certificate they can print out to prove they got through it.

I exaggerate, obviously, but only slightly. If you've ever experienced it, you'll know exactly what I mean. This type of training is usually chosen because a company bought a corporate licence for a training platform that imposes this standard format. From an organisational perspective, the platform makes training easy to organise, easy to distribute. and allows easy tracking of which employees have completed their training. None of these considerations has any bearing on whether the training is effective. Unless, of course, what you deem effective is having an audit trail that shows some training has been delivered. In that case, it'll do exactly what you want.

From the user's perspective, this standard format means every training course looks and feels the same. When you think about it, it makes no sense if our objective is for people to genuinely understand and remember what they're being taught. We know this from school. You wouldn't try to teach chemistry and history in the same classroom using the same techniques. If we want people to learn, then we need to think about the outcome we're looking to achieve.

One of the other differences between school and work is that what we learn at school is typically geared towards an examination. On some level, we're being taught a syllabus, on which we can then be tested to demonstrate competence in and understanding of a particular subject.

Ultimately, schoolchildren will need to pass an exam. Whereas in a work environment, there are many different reasons you might want to train people, not all of them require or merit an exam at the end. To illustrate this, I will explore three simple examples of why we might want to train people in a work environment:

1. Awareness
2. Understanding
3. Autonomy

These examples are common issues employees might need to respond to at an unpredictable time. This will help to illustrate that not all training outcomes are the same:

Awareness

The first outcome we might want is to make our employees aware of a particular dynamic. We just need them to understand a topic enough to recognise something if and when they come across it. If all we want people to do is report something if they see it – for example, they suspect money laundering may be taking place – then all they need is enough information to allow them to do that. At its simplest, they need to know what clues to look for, who to notify, and the fact that they shouldn't tip off the person whose activity they're reporting.

That might require them to have an elementary level of understanding of how money laundering works to spot the telltale signs. But we're not trying to teach them to become money launderers or anti-money-laundering compliance experts!

Understanding

If, on the other hand, we need them to take action if they come across something, then we'll need to give them a greater level of understanding. For example, when it comes to fire prevention, we might want people to report any fires they come across and take basic steps to help contain them.

That might mean training them on how and when to use a fire extinguisher and when they should prioritise personal safety over trying to put the fire out. Because the desired action involves a basic level of decision-making about the risks posed by the fire, the level of knowledge they'll need is more than an awareness of what a fire is. However, just as we weren't trying to teach people how to launder money in the earlier example, here we're not trying to turn people into firefighters.

Autonomy

In other contexts, we'll need people to have a more detailed understanding of a particular topic to make autonomous decisions. An excellent example is first aid training, which aims to equip people with the knowledge and skills to minimise injury and future disability to another person. A trained first aider will need to know how to recognise the difference between a minor injury they can deal with on their own and a more serious one, where their role will be to stabilise the patient until the first responders arrive.

Desired Outcome

As we can see from these simplified examples, there is a big difference between the required outcomes in each case and what the "job" of delivering it might need. First aid – and potentially fire training – necessitate hands-on practical experience in a way that money-laundering awareness does not.

Equally, it is reasonable to assume that people trained in first aid or fire prevention will clearly understand the reason for the training. The same might not be nearly as evident to people attending anti-money-laundering training.

What these examples illustrate is that if we want to ensure we get our desired outcome, we need to think carefully about what that outcome is. In other words, what it is that we want people to do. In the next chapter, we'll see how Behavioural Science can help us to do that.

Note

1. Yuval Feldman, *The Law of Good People* (Cambridge: Cambridge University Press, 2018).

CHAPTER 5
INTRODUCING
BEHAVIOURAL SCIENCE

In this and Chapters 6–8, I introduce some basic Behavioural Science concepts. Readers familiar with the discipline may wish to skip these chapters and move straight to Part II.

Behavioural Science

As a child, my parents always encouraged me to be curious. That meant I constantly asked questions, usually ones that started with the word "why". The primary focus of my questions was an attempt to understand other people and what motivated their behaviour. Why, I would ask, was that person wearing those clothes? Why were those people crossing the road when the traffic light was red? My parents would patiently answer as best they could.

I think childhood curiosity partly led me to study French and German literature at university. I didn't know it then, but in hindsight, the fact that literature explores humans and their decisions attracted me to that field of study. We don't write stories about objects; we write them about people. Or, in the case of fairy tales, we sometimes write them about animals or creatures that are anthropomorphised; in other words, given human characteristics. I was, and remain, particularly fascinated by authors such as Sartre and Kafka, whose stories reveal much about the human brain and why we make choices.

As you'll have detected in the way I told the Cullinan and Adoboli stories in the Introduction, that curiosity hasn't gone away. I'm still fascinated by what makes people "tick". This is why when I first heard about something called "Behavioural

Science", it intrigued me because it seemed to provide some answers. Behavioural Science – or "BeSci" (pronounced "Bee Sci") as I like to abbreviate it[1] – is the study of the "real" drivers of human decision-making. When I say "real", I mean the actual reasons we do things, as opposed to the reasons we might tell ourselves or others that we've done them.

When I was looking for a way to meet the challenge the Oscars story had set me – that of understanding human decision-making – BeSci provided the answer. It was something I'd been interested in for several years, but I hadn't made the connection with what I was doing at work. If we genuinely wanted to mitigate human risk effectively, it became evident that we should be designing frameworks that reflected the realities of how people actually think, rather than how we would like them to think.

If I wanted to be good at influencing my colleagues at UBS, why not be informed by others who were also in the business of influencing human decision-making?

People like transport authorities, advertisers, and (whisper it) governments. All of them use BeSci to achieve their aims. While an advertisement is an attempt to persuade us to buy a product or service, compliance is an attempt to persuade people to comply with rules. Or, as someone once put it to me, marketing is about getting people to do something, compliance is about getting them not to do it!

Nudge

I first became aware of BeSci in 2008 when a book called *Nudge* came out. Written by Professors Cass Sunstein and Richard Thaler, it had the intriguing subtitle "Improving Decisions About Health, Wealth and Happiness".[2] The simple idea behind nudging is that if you want people to do things, it isn't always necessary to mandate or incentivise them. In the book, they highlighted that by changing the "choice architecture" – in simple terms, the way choices are presented to us – you can influence people's decisions.

If, for example, you want to get children to make healthier choices in a school canteen, you can change how you display the food. By presenting healthier options before unhealthier ones, the children are more likely to fill their plates with vegetables and leave less room for fries. This tactic also works on adults and can be used in various contexts.

The idea behind *Nudge* is that you maintain people's rights to choose what they want but nudge them – rather than shove them – towards making better decisions. Of course, this raises ethical questions about who gets to decide whether something is "better", but as Thaler and Sunstein point out, there is no such thing as "neutral" choice architecture. Whenever we're asked to make a choice, someone has determined the order in which it is presented to us, whether it's a dropdown menu on a website or a list of candidates on a ballot paper.

In the UK, in 2010, the government established something called "The Behavioural Insights Team"[3]– nicknamed "The Nudge Unit" – to put these ideas into practice. Their remit was to conduct experiments that tested whether there were ways of persuading people to do things like pay their taxes on time, eat more healthily, and insulate their homes, not just using nudging but a range of BeSci techniques.

Thinking Fast and Slow

Then, in 2011, Professor Daniel Kahneman published a seminal book called *Thinking, Fast and Slow*.[4] You may already own a copy; it's a bestseller. If you do and haven't finished reading it, you'll be pleased to hear you're not alone. In a mock piece of research undertaken in 2014, mathematician Jordan Ellenberg sought to identify the most unread books; things people had purchased but not finished reading.[5] *Thinking, Fast and Slow* came in fourth, with the average reader getting through only 6.8% of the book.

Fortunately, I'm not the average reader, so I can tell you what it says! The book summarised decades of research Kahneman had done into human behaviour with his collaborator Amos Tversky. If you're interested in reading more about that, I highly recommend *The Undoing Project* by Michael Lewis.[6]

In *Thinking, Fast and Slow*, Kahneman, who later won a Nobel Prize, explains some of the brain's inner workings and how it takes decisions. The key concept in the book, which gives rise to the title, is that we use two different systems to think. He refers to System 1 – the "fast" brain in *Thinking, Fast and Slow* – and System 2, the "slow" brain. These are not like "left brain" and "right brain"; they are just two different ways our brain takes decisions.

Because it's hard to remember which is System 1 and which is System 2 and easy to confuse them, I prefer the formulation deployed by Dr Zoe Chance of Yale

University in her book *Influence Is Your Superpower*.[7] She takes the same concepts and explains them in a way that is far easier to remember. She refers to System 1 as "the Gator" and System 2 as "the Judge".

The simple idea behind the Gator and the Judge is as follows. If you've ever encountered an alligator, you'll know that it is an animal that reacts instinctively to things. It's a "shoot first, ask questions later" type of creature, though, for obvious reasons, they tend not to ask any. Meanwhile, judges are almost the exact opposite. They take their time to deliberate on matters and think carefully about them before pronouncing judgement.

Chance explains it as follows: "The Gator is responsible for every cognitive process that's quick and requires little attention. This includes emotions, snap judgements, pattern recognition, and any behaviour that has become easy or habitual through practice." Meanwhile, the Judge "is responsible for every cognitive process requiring concentration and effort".

Here's a simple example that illustrates when we're using our Gator brain and when we're using the Judge. If I ask you what 2×2 is, you'll be able to tell me straight away. If I ask you what 17×67 is, then most of you will have to spend time thinking about it. The first question is not only a straightforward calculation we'll have committed to memory from a young age, but it's also something we use daily without even realising it. Lots of things we buy come in 2×2 formats; yoghurt pots and cans of beer, for example. The quick recall comes courtesy of our Gator brain.

The second question is a lot harder. We tend not to need to multiply things by 17 or 67 times. It's not an answer we've ever needed to commit to memory because it's not something we're likely to need. Most of you will have felt a delay as you worked out the answer. That's the Judge brain in action. In keeping with judicial tradition, it likes to think before producing a response. This doesn't just apply to maths problems. It's also the way we make other decisions.

Cognitive Biases and Heuristics

On the face of it, the Gator and the Judge sounds like a compelling pairing. But – you knew there was a "but" coming! – there are some problems with it. I'll leave it to Harvard Professor Dan Gilbert to explain. Here's what he said in a fascinating TED Talk titled, "Why We Make Bad Decisions".[8]

Our brains were evolved for a very different world than the one in which we are living... in which people lived in very small groups, rarely met anybody who was terribly different from themselves, had rather short lives in which there were few choices, and the highest priority was to eat and mate today.

It's another way of describing what evolutionary psychologists sometimes call the Four F's: fighting, fleeing, feeding and ... procreation. Given those simple priorities, the brain we have is perfectly adequate. If all you need to do is survive, then an algorithm that prioritises efficient decision-making is all you need. In that world, you'll never need to know what 17 × anything is. However, given the challenges we face in the twenty-first century, it's got some severe limitations.

One is that the Gator uses shortcuts to make quicker decisions. There are two kinds – I'll use their technical names so that if you want to do more research, you'll know what to look for – cognitive biases and heuristics.

Cognitive biases are decision-making processes that are baked into the human operating system. A good example is "hindsight bias", where we assume that things are far more predictable than they were in reality. Remember when I said that "in hindsight", one of the reasons I'd studied literature was because I was a curious child? It makes a good story, but I have no way of knowing whether that's true. I've created a narrative that makes what happened sound inevitable and obvious.

On the other hand, a heuristic is a "rule of thumb" that we've learned from experience, which we use to help us make decisions. A good example of a heuristic is something I've learned while riding motorbikes. If you see a parked vehicle and the wheels are pointing out into the traffic, there's a strong likelihood the driver is about to pull out. It's reasonably accurate because most people park their vehicles with the wheels pointing forwards. For motorcyclists, this heuristic is a potential lifesaver since there's a very high chance that the driver of that vehicle won't have seen you. Incidentally, not spotting something obvious because you weren't paying attention is known as "inattentional blindness". Knowing it exists and when it might kick in allows those of us riding bikes to hang back or take a wide berth as we pass.

The cognitive bias and the heuristic I gave as examples aren't exactly nefarious, though I'd understand if the cognitive bias example means you felt misled! But there are plenty of situations where the short cut provided by a cognitive bias or heuristic can deliver a terrible outcome. We only have to think of racism as an example of where prejudiced shortcuts like "people that look different to me are dangerous" can lead to some appalling outcomes.

The Human Algorithm

The other problem with the shortcuts is that we're often not even aware we're using them. You've probably heard the term "unconscious bias". If you're really unlucky, your employer will have sent you on some "unconscious bias" training. I say that not because I'm against the idea of fighting prejudice but because I remain unconvinced that eliminating discrimination is possible by doing a workshop or training course. We should absolutely recognise that prejudice exists, but if it's unconscious, it will take a lot more than a training course to fix it!

OK, so this doesn't sound great, but even if the Gator makes rash decisions, at least we've got the Judge. If only things were that simple! NYU psychologist Professor Jonathan Haidt, the author of *The Righteous Mind*,[9] uses the analogy of the White House in Washington, DC, to explain what's really happening. He says that the rational brain – in other words, the Judge – thinks it's the Oval Office, but it's actually the Press Office. To put it another way, the decisions we believe our brains are making using the Judge are actually being made by the Gator. The Judge's role is to work out how to make the best story out of the decisions already taken elsewhere!

Not at Home to Mr. Logic

What you've hopefully realised by now is that the one thing our brains aren't doing is taking entirely logical decisions. We might get to a good answer that fits a logical model; if that is, the Judge has done their job properly. But what we don't have is an entirely logical process.

I know this because my favourite cartoon character is called Mr Logic.[10] Bear with me here; this will make sense. Mr Logic appears in an adult comic magazine called *Viz*, and he's very amusing. Or rather, the stories in which he features are amusing. The humour comes from the fact that Mr Logic is entirely logical, as his name implies. For example, he takes everything people say to him literally. In one story, someone asks Mr Logic whether he knows how to get to the museum. Rather than providing directions, he responds, "Yes, I do", and promptly ends the conversation. The running joke in the cartoon strip is that in being entirely logical, Mr Logic is extremely dislikable and "non-empathetic". In short, he is not very human.

In another story, Mr Logic is in a town he doesn't know, somewhere in the UK. He approaches a passer-by and asks them for directions, not in English but in Mandarin. Not for the first time, he's made an abysmal choice of who to ask. His logical brain has meant he's picked the first person he's come across. They just happen to be someone of low tolerance and limited intelligence.

Enraged, they ask him why he's speaking to them in a foreign language. Mr Logic explains that since Mandarin is the most spoken language on Earth, and he is in an unfamiliar location, statistically, it is most likely that they will also be a Mandarin speaker. As is often the case, the conversation degenerates into violence; yet again, Mr Logic finds himself in hospital. The cartoon is amusing because it highlights a contradiction in the way our brains work. On the one hand, we all consider ourselves highly logical. On the other hand, we know that many of the decisions we make just aren't.

This means one simple thing: if we want to influence human decision-making, we can't approach it logically. In a work context, if we assume that just because we've written something in a policy, people will read it, understand it, and accept it, we're living in Mr Logic's world and not the real world. Equally, just because we've trained people on a particular rule doesn't mean they'll automatically remember it six months later. Even the best-intentioned people make mistakes and are fallible. We need to think behaviourally.

To achieve this, we will need to understand more about the shortcuts that drive our decision-making and how they work. I like to think of this as a data problem. Since the human OS (operating system) runs an algorithm that we can't reprogram, on hardware that also can't be upgraded, the only thing we can do is to influence the data that it uses. If we change what data goes in, we'll influence the decisions it makes.

Common Cognitive Biases

For the rest of this chapter, I will briefly introduce three of the most common types of cognitive biases pervasive in human thinking. I've chosen categories particularly relevant to human risk; names of relevant biases are listed in parentheses in case you want to learn more.

1. The time bias

2. The loss bias

3. The action bias

The first category of biases I want to highlight is those that relate to time. These biases helped us meet an evolutionary need for what we might today describe as "instant gratification". If we can have something today, then it's better than having it tomorrow. After all, our ancestors couldn't be sure they would be around the next day. That means we can find ourselves prioritising smaller short-term gains over larger long-term ones. If you've ever paid a premium to have something that isn't urgent dispatched to you more quickly, you know all about this! (This is present bias.)

The second category relates to losses and again has an evolutionary explanation. In a world of scarce resources, our ancestors wanted to protect what they had because that was more certain than the chance of them being able to get more. This means we tend to focus more energy on avoiding losses than making gains, even when the amounts involved are the same. If you've ever lost a £20 note, you'll know that the pain you feel will exceed the joy you get from finding a £20 note. (This is loss aversion.)

The third category relates to action and the natural tendency we have to prefer action over inaction. If there are two alternatives, one involves taking action, and the other involves doing nothing, we are more likely to want to do something than not. (This is action bias.)

A wonderful German word highlights what can happen due to a bias towards action: verschlimmbessern. It's when we try to improve things, but in doing so, we actually make them worse.

The Three Drivers

In the following chapters, I will introduce you to the three of the most significant drivers of human decision-making. These are:

1. Our experience and knowledge.

2. What we see or believe other people are doing or thinking.

3. The context in which we are making the decision.

It's not an exhaustive list, but they'll give you a good idea of some key levers we can pull when trying to influence our employees' decision-making. They'll also help you to understand how your employees are likely to react when you ask them to comply with your rules. If you bear all three in mind, you've got a good chance of identifying some of the main reasons behind their decisions.

Each driver has cognitive biases that are associated with it. We'll cover a few of those as we explore the driver and why it helps shape our decisions. None of the drivers operates in isolation; they're just inputs to the human algorithm. Which one takes precedence will depend on the individual situation. To that extent, we should think of them as a cocktail of drivers; the nature of the situation determines the exact mix.

With that said, let's explore the first driver: our own experience and knowledge.

Notes

1. For obvious reasons, I don't like abbreviating it to "BS"!

2. Richard Thaler and Cass Sunstein, *Nudge: Improving Decisions about Health, Wealth, and Happiness* (New Haven, CT: Yale University Press, 2008).

3. https://humanizingrules.link/bi

4. Daniel Kahneman, *Thinking, Fast and Slow* (New York: Farrar, Straus and Giroux, 2012).

5. https://humanizingrules.link/index

6. Michael Lewis, *The Undoing Project* (New York: Penguin Books, 2017).

7. Zoe Chance, *Influence Is Your Superpower: The Science of Winning Hearts, Sparking Change, and Making Good Things Happen* (New York: Random House, 2022).

8. https://humanizingrules.link/gilbert

9. Jonathan Haidt, *The Righteous Mind: Why Good People Are Divided by Politics and Religion* (New York: Pantheon Books, 2012).

10. https://humanizingrules.link/logic

CHAPTER 6
BEHAVIOURAL DRIVER 1: OUR EXPERIENCE AND KNOWLEDGE

Invisible Ink

In 1995, a large middle-aged man called McArthur Wheeler robbed two Pittsburgh banks at gunpoint in broad daylight. Unusually for a bank robber, Wheeler didn't wear a mask or any form of disguise. He even smiled at the surveillance cameras. Unsurprisingly, he was arrested later that day. When the police showed him the video tapes of him robbing the banks, Wheeler couldn't understand how they had managed to find him. "But I wore the juice," he told them. It transpired that Wheeler had discovered that you could make invisible ink using lemon juice. He had then taken his newfound knowledge and, for some reason, concluded that it would also serve to make him invisible. Having covered his face with it, he thought he had the perfect disguise.

Two academics, David Dunning and Justin Kruger, read about the story and were intrigued. How, they wondered, could someone be quite so stupid? Dunning and Kruger decided to find out and undertook some research. What they discovered – later published under the title "Unskilled and unaware of it"[1] – was a cognitive bias called the Dunning–Kruger Effect. In simple terms, it's the idea that unskilled people make poor decisions. Their incompetence also means they lack sufficient "metacognitive ability" – what you and I might call intelligence – to realise it.

The Dunning–Kruger Effect is pervasive. For extreme examples of it, I recommend visiting the Darwin Awards website.[2] It's an annual competition which seeks to "commemorate individuals who protect our gene pool by making the ultimate sacrifice of their own lives. Darwin Award winners eliminate themselves

49

in an extraordinarily idiotic manner, thereby improving our species' chances of long-term survival."

While the Dunning–Kruger Effect is obviously not something you'll ever want to find yourself demonstrating, it's a good illustration of the first and most significant driver of human decision-making: our experience and knowledge. We might not rely on it to botch bank robberies, but we do to guide other choices we make.

The Importance of Experience

Think of a significant decision you've taken recently – something like which car to buy. For excellent reasons, you'll have relied on your experience to help you. If you've had a good or bad experience with a particular car brand, you'll factor that into your decision. Equally, it'll inform which features you want and which you can live without.

The same logic applies to more minor decisions, like what food you will eat for dinner. Experience with a particular cuisine is highly relevant information regarding your current decision. It might not always be evident to us, but we rely heavily on our experience. Otherwise, we'd struggle to complete relatively complex tasks like crossing the road.

In McArthur Wheeler's case, it clearly wasn't past experience of using invisible ink to hide his face that guided his decision, or he would have realised the flaw in his not-so-cunning plan. But he was relying on something he had learned in the past, an expertise Wheeler thought he'd developed in making invisible ink.

We cannot know how good Wheeler's knowledge of invisible ink was. Perhaps he had become an advanced student in invisible ink-making, and the only thing that let him down was that he'd tried to apply his expert skills to a domain where they weren't relevant. It seems incredibly unlikely. In his case, it's more likely that a little bit of knowledge was a dangerous thing.

Evolution

One of the lessons from the Dunning–Kruger research is that we can all misjudge our expertise. It doesn't just apply to those who go on TV talent shows thinking they can sing when it is clear they can't. On some level, it's all of us. There's an evolutionary explanation for this.

To ensure their survival in a challenging environment, our ancestors developed high confidence in their decision-making. Self-doubt is, after all, not a helpful attribute in a hunter-gatherer society. In the relatively simple world they inhabited – the one described by that Dan Gilbert quote in Chapter 5 – it made sense to rely on decisions they'd made in the past to guide the ones they were making in the present.

Not least because in a world where you're living from day to day, if you were in a position where you had to make a decision you'd previously made, it meant that the result of that decision had been that you were still alive. In a world of short life expectancy, it is probably a good indicator of a high-quality decision.

Confirmation Bias

Unfortunately, that's not always a helpful attribute in the modern world. Sometimes it's merely a little unhelpful, but at other times, it can lead us to poor decisions. For example, at the more harmless end of the spectrum, it means seeking validation for decisions we've already made.

If, like me, you've ever bought a product and then read reviews of it after making your purchase, you'll be aware of something called *confirmation bias*. It's a cognitive bias that helps us to minimise the amount of information we need to process by filtering out information that doesn't support our current thinking. So, when we read those reviews after purchasing, we like the ones that support our decision and reject the ones that don't.

More dangerously, it can mean taking decisions where we filter out all information that contradicts our pre-existing beliefs. We might go through the motions of making a balanced assessment, but, in reality, our mind is already made up. The risk of being blind to new information that should lead us to question our pre-existing beliefs is evident, particularly in a rapidly changing environment. Of course, self-belief can be a great thing that empowers us to develop new skills and be successful. But, as McArthur Wheeler discovered, if those existing beliefs are wrong, they can also be highly dangerous.

Agency, or the Coat Problem

Self-belief also helps to support another common human trait: our desire *to be in control*.

That question you always asked your parents – or if you've got kids, will find yourself being asked – five minutes after setting out on a long journey, "Are we nearly there, yet?", isn't just about boredom. It's also a desire for a sense of control.

If we don't know what's going on, we feel as if we have no control. This is why websites use progress bars on things like customer surveys or downloads; If we know how long something will take, we feel more in control.

Those of you with kids will recognise what I call the "coat problem". Telling children to wear a coat can often result in them refusing to do so, even if they were going to wear one anyway. How you can deal with that, by the way, is to reframe the discussion. Start off by saying, "It's cold, you're obviously going to want to wear a coat. Which coat would you like to wear?" Magically, that will make them feel like they're in control and have a sense of ownership. And they're far more likely to wear a coat.

Repetition Suppression

One of the other ways we limit the amount of information we need to process is to ignore things we've seen before and focus on new things. The first time we encounter something, we pay close attention to it as we try to figure out what it means.

If you've ever learned a new word and then kept hearing it, you've experienced something called the *Baader-Meinhof effect*. The name comes from a left-wing German terrorist group active in the 1970s to the 1990s. A poster on an internet discussion board in the US in the early 1990s had heard the name – which wasn't something they would typically expect to hear – twice in 24 hours and wondered why. You'll experience something similar if you've just bought or are looking at purchasing a new car. The model you've purchased or are interested in will seem to be very common. It's not. You're just noticing it more than you notice other models. Now that I've told you about Baader-Meinhof you may well find it cropping up far more.

The flip side of this extra focus is that we spend less time looking at things we already understand. This is known as *repetition suppression*. The more familiar we are with something, the less we need to focus on it. That's why, for example, you may find yourself on autopilot when commuting to and from work or making a journey you complete regularly. There's no need for your brain to focus on something you know well.

The downside of repetition suppression is that we can quickly get used to things. That's great if the thing we're getting used to is a positive outcome. But it can also apply to bad habits. In the context we're exploring, it can mean that people who start breaking the rules will get used to them and may not even notice they're doing it.

The Curse of Knowledge

Another consequence of repetition suppression is taking pieces of information we already have for granted. Once we know something, we find it hard to imagine not understanding it. That makes it difficult for us to put ourselves in the shoes of other people who don't have that knowledge.

If you've ever seen someone who is an expert in a field struggling to explain things to someone who isn't, then you'll recognise this dynamic. Some talented sports professionals don't make good coaches because they can't imagine not having their abilities.

This is a cognitive bias known as the *curse of knowledge*. It's a curse because although we have the knowledge, it also serves to blind us to the fact that other people don't. This can be problematic if, for example, we need to train other people or write rules for them. In both cases, we are likely to make presumptions about the level of knowledge of the people we're training or writing rules for them that might not be correct.

It's a problem that can be exacerbated when the subject matter is particularly complex or the frequency in which employees engage with it is low. In those cases, the gap between what the expert knows and is familiar with and what the general population knows and is familiar with is far greater. Someone who spends all their time working on an annual attestation or reporting process may, for understandable reasons, struggle to appreciate the level of understanding of someone who doesn't.

Sunk Cost Fallacy

The final cognitive bias I want to highlight for this driver is the *sunk cost fallacy*. This is a natural tendency that we can have to be reluctant to abandon a course of action because we have invested heavily in it. It occurs even when it is clear that giving up on the path of action would be better for us.

One explanation is that if we have invested time or money in a particular plan, we like to stick with that plan. Like McArthur Wheeler, we back ourselves to be right and therefore assume that if we've invested in something, it must be a good idea. We can see this playing out in investment strategies – where people are reluctant to sell positions they have held for some time – and in political or strategic decisions, where people stick to plans, even where it is evident the plan is not working.

When it comes to influencing our employees, it can lead us to deploy strategies that don't work but that we have always used. If, for example, we think training is the solution to our employees not doing what we want, then our response to something going wrong is to add more training. We don't stop to think about whether training is the correct answer because that's our standard strategy.

Implications for Humanizing Rules

What all of these biases have in common is that they drive us towards self-belief. In other words, the experience and knowledge we have gained will always be appropriate in solving our problems. From an evolutionary perspective, this makes perfect sense. For people living in the twenty-first century, it poses substantial risks. If we're blind to different perspectives and stick rigidly to how we've always done things, we'll likely make mistakes.

Basing decisions on experience means that we risk replicating poor choices we have made in the past. Just because something worked before, or seems to have worked before, doesn't mean it was the right decision. We must just have been lucky. Nor does it mean it's the right decision for the present situation. Even if it was the right decision in the past, there's the risk that the current situation is different in some way that we might not recognise and that, therefore, the past solution isn't appropriate.

When thinking about the challenges of humanizing rules, it's important to remember that these biases apply to our employees and to us. That means we must consider two different dynamics when thinking about how to mitigate human risk and maximise human reward. The first is how our employees will likely respond to what we're asking them to do. The second is how we react to that. Biases will probably kick in, not just in how they behave but in how we seek to influence them.

Now that we've looked at the most significant driver of human behaviour – our own experience and knowledge – we'll move on to look at a second one, the influence that other people have on us, in Chapter 7.

Notes

1. David Dunning and Justin Kruger, "Unskilled and unaware of it: How difficulties in recognizing one's own incompetence lead to inflated self-assessments", *Journal of Personality and Social Psychology*, 77 (1999): 1121–1134.

2. www.darwinawards.com

CHAPTER 7
BEHAVIOURAL DRIVER 2: OTHER PEOPLE

The Shed

If you've ever found yourself in an unfamiliar city needing somewhere to eat, chances are you've looked at a site like Tripadvisor for restaurant reviews. But how much can we rely on what those sites tell us? Less than we might think if the experience of London-based lifestyle and food writer Oobah Butler is anything to go by. In 2017, Butler was repeatedly given money to write positive reviews on Tripadvisor for restaurants in which he'd never eaten.

Since this was happening frequently, he wondered why. Butler noticed that, for some reason, his reviews, in particular, were a catalyst that could shoot restaurants up the Tripadvisor rankings. So, in a mischievous mood, he conducted an experiment. Butler set out to see if he could get a non-existent restaurant to the No. 1 ranking on Tripadvisor. Re-naming his backyard shed in Dulwich as a restaurant called "The Shed", he created a logo, built a website and listed the restaurant as "by appointment only" so he didn't need to give an address or serve anyone a meal.

Using fake reviews and the pretence of being fully booked for months in advance, The Shed climbed from 18,149 in the Tripadvisor London rankings to number one.[1] While Butler's experimental prank clearly raises some ethical questions, it's also the perfect illustration of the power of the second behavioural driver: other people.

The Wisdom of the Crowd

We turn to Tripadvisor and similar websites for help because we instinctively know that other people are a good source of insight. That's not a dynamic that

Tripadvisor has created, it's always been there. Long before the days of review websites, we would have relied on other people to guide us in situations where we had limited knowledge.

On holiday, we might have asked the concierge or front desk for a restaurant recommendation. Or, we might have consulted our guidebook. Tripadvisor just takes this to a whole new level by allowing us to tap into the wisdom of a vast crowd. It's the size of that crowd that is also what makes us more willing to trust the site.

By aggregating many reviews, Tripadvisor also helps us mitigate the risk of making a wrong decision. If we were just to ask one person, we might not get a representative view. Accessing a broader perspective means we can mitigate the risk of being swayed by outliers.

Behavioural Contagion

The idea that we allow ourselves to be influenced by the opinions and actions of others is something we intuitively understand.

There's a reason parents warn their children about falling in with the wrong crowd. They know that the behaviour of those whose company we keep influences our own. In *Under the Influence*, Professor Robert Frank explains that "by far the strongest predictor of whether someone will smoke is the percentage of her closest friends who smoke. If that number rises from 20 to 30, for example, the probability that she will smoke rises by about 25 percent."[2]

Given that example, this sounds like bad news. It helps to explain the "if you can't beat them, join them" attitude shown by many people during the COVID pandemic when they panic-bought toilet rolls in industrial quantities.

But there's also an upside. As Professor Frank explains in his book, we can also use these social forces for good. Turning his smoking statistic on its head, if we can reduce the number of the closest friends who smoke from 30 to 20, the probability she will smoke reduces by 25 percent.

They Must Know Something I Don't

One of the reasons we copy other people is because we assume that if they're engaging in a particular behaviour, there must be a valid reason. They must know something we don't. And, of course, very often, they do. You'll recognise this when you go to a city or a country you've never been to before. You work out how to behave by copying what other people do. Whether that's working out how much to tip the staff or whether you need to tip them at all. Whether it's okay to cross the road when the lights are red or whether you have to wait for the lights to change.

And, of course, there's a logic to that. In the case of our restaurant choice, the other option we have is to use a very simple heuristic: go and see where other people are eating. We don't want to get ripped off, poisoned, or suffer lousy service. Nor do they. So we can minimise risk by avoiding places that no one else seems to want to eat in. We don't even need to know why a restaurant is empty. We just know that if it is, we're better off not eating there.

Conversely, if we find somewhere that lots of other people are happy going to, we've minimised the chance of a poor choice, providing that the people we're copying are locals who know what they're doing rather than tourists who might not.

Social Proof

The second reason that copying others makes sense is that we're naturally social creatures. And if we want to be accepted by other people, then the best way to do that is to behave the way they do. If we mimic their behaviours, they will be drawn to us, and we're more likely to be taken into the group. We also know intuitively that people who stand out face ridicule or social exclusion. Conformity comes naturally to us. We take comfort from feeling part of a group because it gives us a sense of identity. Anyone who's a sports fan will recognise the bond that builds between supporters of the same team and the hostility that grows against fans of the opposing team. Equally, if you've ever experienced *groupthink* in a meeting, you'll know how easily we can coalesce around a common position when we're in a group.

From an evolutionary perspective, there's safety in numbers. Far better to go with the flow than to run the risk of being an outlier who can be picked off by a predator. If the herd moves, we should probably move with it for our own protection. That's often the case when herd mentality manifests itself on an individual level; what is known as *social proof*, where we permit ourselves to do things because we know that's what others are doing. Taking comfort from the fact other people are doing something feels safe. And it can make a lot of sense. But it can also end up with us doing things that aren't in our best interest.

Businesses are adept at using social proof to persuade us to part with our money. Very often, that involves using existing customers to attract new ones. Restaurants that depend on passing trade will often fill "visible" seats first – those by the window or outside – so the people passing get a sense that the place is popular. Nightclubs have to adopt a slightly different approach. Since they can't show you inside the club – there are, after all, no windows – they will artificially create a line outside, even when they don't need to. That way, anyone passing will think the place must be incredibly popular because people are prepared to wait to go in!

The idea of making things that are normally invisible, visible is also used in other contexts. I once visited British Airways (BA) to find out how airlines manage risk and picked up copy of their staff magazine. In a prominent place, where you would ordinarily expect to see corporate messaging, there was a column called "Mistake of the Month", where an employee would write about a mistake they had made and what they'd learned from it.

Obviously, it was curated; it wasn't "I got drunk last night and still managed to land the plane in Malaga" type stories. Instead, it was things like "I'm responsible for the buses that take staff around the airport and we realised that we'd introduced a route that no one would ever want to travel on so we cancelled it and saved a million pounds."

This was a deliberate strategy to normalise talking about mistakes. As Alex Cruz, the then CEO of BA, explained in a magazine interview:[3]

I want people to know it's OK to make a mistake and it's OK to talk about it, because that's how we actually learn. I'm having a tough time getting people to actually admit their mistakes. We have to go and look at them. There's 45,000 people in the company [and] no one makes a mistake? Come on!

The aim of the column wasn't to share details of the mistakes that people had made. It was to normalise the idea of talking about them. Cruz could have told his staff that it was OK to share their mistakes. Instead, he chose to show them that it was.

Negative Social Proof

Perhaps unsurprisingly, social proof doesn't just work one way. Sometimes attempts to show how popular something is can fail miserably if they reveal something is unpopular. This is known as *negative social proof*. Usually, it is provided entirely by accident.

A widespread example of negative social proof is when people running surveys send emails to encourage more people to fill them in. A message like "32% of you have filled in the survey, please can everyone else?" might seem like a good idea. Until you think about the fact that the message also makes it clear that 68% of the population – a vast majority – haven't. Even if the email doesn't contain numbers, phrases like "a large number of you" can have the same effect; the fact that the email has been sent out also sends a signal. You wouldn't send the email if there wasn't a problem big enough to warrant it.

The intended message is "we need your help, please fill the survey in". The subliminal and arguably more powerful statement is "don't bother, hardly anyone else has filled the survey in". It highlights something the email recipients wouldn't otherwise have been aware of. After all, you don't know how many others have completed a digital task until you're told.

That's bad enough, but it gets worse if you think about the impact this type of message will have on those who *have* filled in the survey; there's a risk that they think, "why did I bother when most people haven't?" Unless it is only sent to non-respondents, you risk making them feel silly for being part of a compliant minority when everyone else hasn't complied.

If this is something you see in your organisation, don't worry, there's a simple solution available. It uses something called *framing*, which we'll explore in Chapter 8. Rather than sending a "chaser" email that makes it sound like you are desperate for people to fill in your survey, make it seem like an exclusive, limited-time opportunity to provide feedback. It won't persuade everyone to respond, but it should improve the numbers.

Blind Carbon Copy

Negative social proof can also be seen in other forms of "chaser" emails. Often, when people have failed to complete an exercise on time – for example, they've failed to do mandatory training – an email is sent to that group telling them they need to complete it. For administrative convenience, it is sent to the entire group simultaneously. As a result, the whole group of noncompliant individuals is suddenly made aware of everyone else who has also failed to complete it.

Suddenly, rather than feeling like the one person who hasn't done the training, they've received written confirmation that they're part of a group. A group will feel much larger than it actually is because that's all they can see. So, if 30 people haven't done the training, but hundreds have, all they'll see is the 30, which feels sizeable even if it is only a tiny minority.

If the recipient list contains "influencers" – for example, people in leadership positions – then that can legitimise the idea that not responding is acceptable. Other recipients may feel they are in good company and there's even less need to do the training.

Is this happening in your company? Suggest to the people doing it that they either send out individual emails – ideally making them look personalised – or use "bcc", which hides recipients' names. Alternatively, if the number of people who haven't complied is small enough, why not call them rather than emailing? Since chaser emails are prevalent, receiving a phone call may have a much more significant impact.

Messengers

One of the lessons of the second story I shared about Mr Logic is his failure to assess the appropriateness of the person he asks for help. You'll remember that he's lost, needs directions, and asks the first person he comes across, who is eminently unsuited to the task. From a logical perspective, it doesn't matter who you ask as long as they have the requisite information.

Yet from a practical perspective, that makes no sense at all. There are clearly people whom it makes more sense to ask for help, either because they are more likely to know something or because they are more likely to respond positively to our request.

The same dynamic plays in reverse. When we hear messages, we pay close attention to the messenger. We can interpret the same thing said by two different people entirely differently. If you've ever been in a meeting and suggested something that was roundly ignored, only for someone else to say exactly the same thing and be praised, you'll be aware of this.

If a politician we like suggests something, we may view it differently than a politician we don't like, suggesting the same thing. It's a subject explored in detail in *Messengers: Who We Listen To, Who We Don't, and Why* by Stephen Martin and Joseph Marks.[4] They explain:

Change doesn't necessarily come about as a result of the content or wisdom of the message being communicated. Instead it often comes about as a result of who is delivering the message.

It's why celebrity endorsements are so powerful, providing, of course, we like the person doing the endorsing. From a logical perspective, this makes no sense whatsoever. After all, the fact that a celebrity likes – or is paid to pretend to like – a product doesn't mean it is any good or right for us. Singer Britney Spears is unlikely to have any expertise in making perfumes, yet "Curious" – just *one* of the many ranges she helps to promote – has sold over 500 million bottles.

There's a simple lesson here: if our message isn't getting through to our employees, it might not be the message; it might be the messenger.

Implications for Humanizing Rules

We can see from these biases that the effect other people have on human decision-making can vary. On the one hand, it can be a force for good. On the other, it encourages us to do things we shouldn't. The problem is that we might not be capable of recognising which it is!

The most obvious implication is that we need to remember that the propensity of our employees to follow, bend, or break the rules will be heavily influenced by other people. Therefore, it is essential to recognise where social dynamics are likely to play a vital role in identifying where we can use them – for example, deploying social proof – and where monitoring might be appropriate.

It's time to examine the third driver of human decision-making – context and environment in Chapter 8.

Notes

1. https://humanizingrules.link/shed

2. Robert Frank, *Under the Influence* (Princeton, NJ: Princeton University Press, 2020).

3. https://humanizingrules.link/ba

4. Stephen Martin and Joseph Marks, *Messengers: Who We Listen To, Who We Don't, and Why* (New York: Random House, 2019).

CHAPTER 8
BEHAVIOURAL DRIVER 3: CONTEXT

Is It a Television, or Is It a Bike?

When Amsterdam-based bicycle manufacturer VanMoof began shipping its bikes to the US, they discovered that many were arriving in a damaged state. Not only was this annoying for customers, but it was costing VanMoof a lot of money. So, they tried obvious things like changing their shipping partner and using more robust packaging. But nothing worked.

How, they wondered, was it possible to ship fragile items like televisions in a similar-sized box without them getting damaged, but not bicycles? That question inspired an idea. What if they looked at the problem differently? Rather than trying to protect the box's contents, why not see if they could persuade the handlers to be more careful with them? That thinking led to an experiment. VanMoof put an image of a flatscreen TV on the side of their boxes, hoping that this would make the handlers take more care. It worked, and shipping damages dropped by 70–80%.[1]

For obvious reasons, VanMoof didn't talk about what they'd done. But soon, customers were sharing details of it on social media, and other bike manufacturers borrowed the idea. All of which, ironically, helped make it less effective! It's probably why VanMoof no longer ships bikes with pictures of TVs on the box – they've since found other ways of solving the problem – but the story lives on.

VanMoof's innovative idea perfectly illustrates the final driver of human behaviour: context. How we make decisions is heavily impacted by the context or environment in which we are making them.

Context Matters

We all understand the idea intuitively. It is, for example, perfectly acceptable for me to walk around at home just wearing my underpants. If I did the same thing in a supermarket, I'd be asked to leave and risk being arrested. The same behaviour in one context can be entirely unacceptable in another.

The COVID pandemic also provided an interesting illustration of this. The delineation between "home" and "office" became blurred thanks to lockdowns as people turned the former into the latter. Suddenly behaviours that might have been deemed unacceptable in an office – for example, bringing pets and children into meetings – became normalised. Not to mention the shift in dress codes, as many people wore things for video calls that they probably would not have worn to the office.

Passenger Experience

Transport authorities are very good at understanding the importance of context. London Underground, for example, draws a clear distinction between three phases of a journey: (1) before passengers cross the barriers to go into the station; (2) when they are on a platform waiting to board a train; and (3) when they are on a particular train. They do this, because they know that the information passengers will care about at each stage of their journey is very different.

Before they go through the ticket barrier, passengers still have the choice of aborting or re-routing their journey via alternative routes. The information that matters to them at this point is how the overall network is running and if there are any disruptions. Passengers who need to connect with other lines will then know how their entire journey is likely to pan out.

This is not just important from a practical perspective, it also matters from a psychological one. To understand what information they will find helpful requires an appreciation of the level of commitment they have made to their journey at each stage. Up until they pass the ticket barrier, they still have the option of aborting or re-routing. Once passengers cross the ticket barriers, they have "paid", are "locked" in the system and mentally "committed" to completing their planned trip.

Having reached a platform, passengers then want to know when the next train is due to arrive. They are far less interested in how the network as a whole is operating, and more interested in the specific line they are now on. If that line has problems, they still have the option of finding an alternative, so if there are delays, they need information that helps them decide what to do.

As Rory Sutherland explains in his book, *Alchemy*:[2]

The mammalian brain has a deep-set preference for control and certainty. The single best investment ever made by the London Underground in terms of increasing passenger satisfaction was not to do with money spent on faster, more frequent trains – it was the addition of dot matrix displays on platforms to inform travellers of the time outstanding before the next train arrived.

It's a really simple and relatively cheap solution to reduce passenger anxiety. We'll happily wait for ten minutes if we have certainty that a train is coming. If we don't know when – or, indeed, whether – a train is coming, we'll start to get anxious very quickly, particularly in a confined space like an underground station. Anxious passengers can easily take their anxiety out on members of staff or fellow passengers, so keeping people informed isn't just about maintaining passenger satisfaction.

Once they board a train, passengers are "trapped" and the information that interests them is now what is going to happen to "their train". At this point, the driver is their only source of information, so London Underground has a very simple rule. If a train is stopped outside a station for more than, I believe, 90 seconds – that's the time after which people begin to get anxious – the driver is required to say something. And here's the clever part: they don't get a script. Within reason, they can say whatever they like. That might be "I don't know what's going on, but I'm going to find out" or "I can see there's a train still waiting at the next station, I'm sure we'll be moving shortly."

Context needn't mean physical location. It can also refer to the data that we use to make decisions. As we saw when looking at the Gator and the Judge in Chapter 5, the data that we have available to us impacts the decisions that we take.

What You See Is All There Is

In his book, *Thinking, Fast and Slow*,[3] Daniel Kahneman introduces a concept called WYSIATI, which is short for "What You See Is All There Is". It relates to our ability to make decisions quickly and the data that we use to do so. Kahneman explains that System 1 (i.e., the Gator brain) "is radically insensitive to both the quality and quantity of the information that gives rise to impressions and intuitions".

In other words, when we need to make a decision, we'll grab whatever data we have to hand and use that. As a result, we don't think to look for information that we could or should have to make the best possible decision. Note Kahneman's reference to "impressions" and "intuitions". He isn't just saying that we can sometimes use "dodgy data" when making decisions, but that it can also pollute our gut instincts. The dodgy data isn't just used for a one-off decision; it can stick with us. This partly helps to explain how conspiracy theories and cults take such a hold on people.

As Kahneman goes on to explain:

It is the consistency of the information that matters for a good story, not its completeness. Indeed, you will often find that knowing little makes it easier to fit everything you know into a coherent pattern.

Which brings us back to McArthur Wheeler's failed bank robbery in Chapter 6. He took basic information about invisible ink and managed to create a narrative in his head that persuaded him he'd planned the perfect heist. It's also what is likely to have made the VanMoof solution so effective. The handlers would have seen the image of a television and not thought to question the box's contents. After all, who puts pictures on a box of something that isn't inside? Once the idea that it was a television was implanted in their minds, their behaviour naturally shifted.

Our ability to use limited data is far more problematic than you might initially think. It's not just individuals who make decisions in this way. It's also a problem for society as a whole. In her eye-opening book, *Invisible Women*,[4] Caroline Criado Perez highlights the astonishing – and yet, when you think about it, obvious – point that in a patriarchal society, there are far fewer data points about women available than there are about men. Historically, more men have occupied positions of power and influence than women. As the summary of her book explains, this has wide-ranging consequences:

Imagine a world where your phone is too big for your hand, where your doctor prescribes a drug that is wrong for your body, where in a car accident you are 47% more likely to be seriously injured, where every week the countless hours of work you do are not recognised or valued. If any of this sounds familiar, chances are that you're a woman.

Framing

Human decision-making isn't just influenced by the quality and quantity of data available to us. How that data is presented or "framed" impacts our perception. Here's a simple illustration of how a question is phrased can change the answer people give. In an opinion poll, before the UK's Brexit vote in 2016, a representative sample of the population responded as follows to two opinion poll questions:

"Do you support reducing the voting age from 18 to 16?"

37% said they were in favour, while 56% were against.

"Do you support giving 16- and 17-year-olds the right to vote?"

52% said they were in favour, while 41% were against.

By asking precisely the same question, framed in two different ways, the pollsters were given two very different answers. Obviously, not everyone who participated in the survey gave different answers. But enough of them did to change the collective outcome.

The idea that we can change people's perspective on an issue by changing how it is presented is known as *framing*. We saw it in action in the VanMoof story. By reframing the problem, they were facing as a psychological rather than physical one, they found an innovative solution. They moved from thinking about the challenge of making the box and bike less vulnerable to damage to changing the handlers' behaviour.

Sometimes the Survey *Is* the Advert

Framing is also used in ways that make us drop our guard. If you've ever done a survey that asked you about advertisements you might have seen in a particular publication, then you might be surprised by what I'm about to tell you. On the face of it, those surveys are there to see how effective a particular brand's advertising campaign has been. They work as follows: you're shown some advertisements for that brand and asked if you remember seeing them. Then you're asked if you can remember seeing any advertisements for competitor brands. In some cases, what you see really is all there is.

But, in some cases, what you're being shown isn't all it might seem. Because the advertisements you're being asked to recall have never been published. The first time they've appeared in public is in the survey. Anyone who says, "Yes" to the question of whether they've seen them before is – let's be polite – misremembering. The survey isn't asking about advertisements. The survey is the advertisement! The point is to make you focus on ads for that particular brand for several minutes in a way you would never otherwise do.

Here's the clever part. The reason they ask about competitor brands, at the end, is all to do with something known as *anchoring*. They want you to think of the product you've just seen as being on a par with the other brands they're naming. That way, when you're next looking to buy something in that category, you'll think of that brand. Because they've anchored your perception of the brand they're advertising in the same class as the competitor brands. Which, when you think about it, is well worth the money they spend on whatever prize draw they've used to entice you into doing the survey!

Anchoring

As the name implies, *anchoring* is about framing a conversation around a particular dynamic. The most obvious example is the price of something. One of the oldest tricks salespeople use is comparing the price of the thing they're trying to sell with more expensive items. If they're selling something for £29.99, then drawing comparisons with products that cost £59.99 makes theirs seem relatively cheap.

As does pointing out how much something used to be on sale for before it was discounted. We've all bought things on special offer and been delighted by how much money we've saved. Yet, when you think about it, the fact that you saved £400 by buying a coat for £250, which was once on sale for £650, is irrelevant. What someone else was prepared to pay for it – or rather, what the retailer put it on sale for initially – is an irrelevant piece of information. What matters is the

£250, the money we've actually spent. Yet, we're very likely to focus far more on the £400 than the £250.

Scarcity

One of the other dynamics that retailers use to encourage us to buy things is scarcity. You only have to look at phrases like "while stocks last" or "offer ends this week" to see this in action. The Fear Of Missing Out (FOMO) is very real, particularly when combined with social proof.

Concert promoters frequently make use of scarcity to drive sales. When a major artist announces a tour, it's very common that they'll do so with just one or two shows per venue. If the promoter is confident there's demand there, it'll be two. If they're not, it'll be one. That way, if demand isn't as high as expected, they've just got to fill a venue on one night, rather than having to manage a half-filled one on two nights.

If the existing dates sell out, a further date is released "by popular demand". That extra date was always available, they just never told us about it! By reducing the supply of tickets originally on offer, they can also create a sense of FOMO which will help to sell tickets more quickly. Then, if they do need to add another date, it's against a backdrop of already having sold out.

What works for concerts can also work for things we want our employees to do. As we'll see later, if you've got something like a survey that you need completed, rather than trying to force everyone to complete it, you may be able to use FOMO instead.

The Video Is the Training

To illustrate how you can use these ideas within your organisation, here's how one of my clients adapted "the survey is the advertisement". He's a senior compliance officer in a medium-sized multinational firm whom we'll call Jorge.

The problem Jorge faced is not uncommon. Certain members of senior management were not paying as much attention to compliance – and, in particular, training – as he would have expected. Rather than forcing compliance training on them, he learned from the Coat Problem in Chapter 6 and asked for their help.

Jorge told them he was filming a training video and needed senior management to talk about their experiences, would they help?

In most cases, they said yes. So he invited them to a recording studio for 30 minutes, explaining that he'd only need around a minute's worth of content, so they'd be covering a range of content. During those 30 minutes he got them to explain, in their own words, why compliance is important to them personally; the best parts were then used in a training final video.

Nothing unusual with that, you might think. Then Jorge explained his thinking to me; "They think they're helping to train staff, which they are. But the video is also training for them." Obviously, if the entire exercise had been a sham, then that would have raised ethical questions, but since Jorge was filming the video anyway and used the clips, I think it's smart.

Implications for Humanizing Rules

As with the other two drivers, we must think about two things: (1) how it impacts our decision-making; and (2) how it affects their decision-making.

What all of these cognitive biases mean for compliance is that we need to think carefully about when we engage with people, how we do it, and the language we use. All of these things can influence how people perceive what we are asking them to do.

As we saw with the opinion poll and the television on the bike packaging, tiny changes can make a big difference in how people perceive things. You might not be doing surveys or dispatching bikes, but when you send an email, how you word it and who sends it can all shift people's perception of it.

Equally, it's worth thinking about language and whether words like "compliance" might frame things in an off-putting manner for the recipient. After all, it's not the most exciting piece of branding ever invented, and sending an email with the words "compliance update" might just make people less, rather than more, willing to read it.

We often frame compliance training by referencing the laws or regulations the training is designed to cover. That feels sensible, but it sends an obvious signal that all we care about is communicating that regulation and that we're only doing it because it's a legal or regulatory requirement. This means people will treat it that way; something the organisation wouldn't normally do, but the law requires it.

Now, that might be fine if it's genuinely a rule that you don't think is that important. But if it's something you want people to really engage with, as more than the box-ticking exercise, then you're better off changing the framing. Changing the context from "we're doing this because we have to" to "we're doing this because we think it's important" can significantly impact how people engage with it.

Notes

1. https://humanizingrules.link/bike

2. Rory Sutherland, *Alchemy* (London: WH Allen, 2019).

3. Daniel Kahneman, *Thinking, Fast and Slow* (New York: Penguin, 2012).

4. Caroline Criado Perez, *Invisible Women* (London: Chatto and Windus, 2019).

PART II
HUMANS

CHAPTER 9
INTRODUCING HUMANS

Why We Need a Framework

So far, I've introduced some basic BeSci concepts and the critical importance of thinking about things from our employees' perspective instead of our own. In this part, I will introduce HUMANS, a practical BeSci framework. HUMANS consists of six elements – one for each letter of the word – that can help us think about things from our employees' perspective. As we have explored in earlier chapters, this is not something that comes naturally to us. HUMANS forces us to consider that alternative perspective and to remove the blinkers that dynamics like the curse of knowledge can bring.

If we've already implemented a particular behavioural intervention, HUMANS can help us understand why our employees are reacting to it in the way they are. If, on the other hand, we are planning a behavioural intervention, it can help us to think about how they are likely to react to it. In both cases, we're trying to understand what might be driving their response to what we're asking them to do.

What Is a Behavioural Intervention?

The HUMANS framework is designed for use with "behavioural interventions" (BIs), which are attempts to influence the decision-making and, therefore, the behaviour of our employees. The purpose of a BI is to help deliver a "desired outcome", something we want our employees to do or not do. For example, we might want them to comply with a particular rule.

The principles and ideas I will outline are designed with employees in mind. However, there is no reason you can't use a version of them to influence other stakeholders, such as regulators or customers.

BIs come in a variety of forms. In simple terms, anything that is designed to influence the decisions made by your employees is a BI. Most obviously, that's policies, rules, training, and communications campaigns. If something is intended to be seen, read, or followed by a human, it's a BI. Equally, it includes things that are partially or wholly designed to deter undesirable behaviour. So, we can see controls, monitoring programmes, incentive structures, and disciplinary processes also as forms of BI.

Dress Code

To illustrate the breadth of what can constitute a BI, let's look at a simple example.

The CEO of Big Company ("BigCo") is deeply concerned by what they see as a "post-lockdown decline in standards" in what employees wear to the office. Their "desired outcome" is getting their staff to dress more appropriately. To achieve this, they've identified ten BIs intended to help solve the problem.

They begin by deciding that BigCo needs a detailed dress code (BI1) and take inspiration from a 44-page policy they remember learning about somewhere.[1] They like round numbers, so 50 pages it is! To ensure compliance, they intend to instruct BigCo's security staff to prevent anyone they see in breach of the code from entering the BigCo offices (BI2). Because standards matter at BigCo, the rules apply to anyone working from home (BI3). For that reason, the CEO will also get BigCo's technology team to use artificial intelligence to monitor adherence to the code during video calls (BI4). Anyone failing to comply with the rules will automatically lose one day's salary (BI5).

Internal comms will email all employees to ensure everyone is aware of this new approach (BI6). They'll also put up posters in the BigCo offices showing the difference between "appropriate" and "inappropriate" attire (BI7).[2] The BigCo CEO also intends to do a video interview for the intranet to talk about their "passion for fashion" and why "smart dress means business success" (BI8). Every employee will also be required to do three hours of a training course called "what to wear at work" (BI9). Finally, BigCo will provide each employee with a $500 voucher – the company will meet all employee tax obligations – that they can spend at a retailer of their choice to buy work clothes (BI10).

Fortunately, I've just described an entirely fictional example that is purely there to illustrate that BIs are a broad concept and the HUMANS framework, therefore, has wide applicability. It's not just for obvious "comms" things like training courses, emails, or posters. We can also consider how employees will or are likely to perceive our entire control environment, including elements like controls.

As well as applying HUMANS to the BIs, we can use it to achieve the desired outcome. In this case, we could ask the simple question of whether the very idea of the CEO imposing dress standards or requirements is something the employees would find reasonable or acceptable. The answer to that question could then determine the selection and design of individual BIs.

Of course, in this case, the example is so extreme that we don't need a framework to tell us that the approach being adopted by our fictional CEO is – I'll be polite here – "overkill". With the obvious exception of the voucher, which seems entirely out of character. Even if employees accepted the idea of imposed dress standards, the way the CEO approaches the problem is unnecessarily aggressive. Setting a dress code requirement and policing it this way are highly likely to breed employee resentment, particularly among the Security and IT teams required to help implement the regime.

There are a couple of ways the BigCo CEO could potentially use HUMANS. The first would have stopped them from implementing some of the more extreme measures while encouraging ideas like the voucher. By using HUMANS as a design tool, they would better understand the likely success of the BIs they were proposing. That way, they could focus on the ones most likely to be effective and either drop or redesign those that are likely to be less effective or even counter-productive.

The second way they could use HUMANS would be if they were reviewing existing BIs. Let's imagine that instead of implementing the new regime, they had inherited it from their predecessor. In that case, they'd be using it as a diagnostic tool to identify areas for improvement. Because the BIs have already been implemented, the CEO would also have behavioural data that they could use to inform the analysis offered by the HUMANS framework.

HUMANS Overview

Each element in the HUMANS framework allows us to think about different aspects of how our employees are likely to perceive what we are imposing on them. By prompting key questions, each element ensures that we consider a range of behavioural dynamics, many of which we might otherwise neglect.

Since we are trying to understand things from the perspective of our employees, the key questions are intentionally framed that way round. So, rather than asking, "How helpful will our employees find what we are asking them to do?", the framework asks, "How helpful do I find what they are asking me to do?"

The framework works on a straightforward premise: if the answer to the key question is positive, then it is more likely – though, of course, by no means guaranteed – that our employees will comply with what we are asking them to do. Conversely, if the answer to the key question is negative, they will be less likely to comply with what we are asking them to do.

If that all sounds rather messy, remember that we're assessing human decision-making, which isn't always straightforward. Human emotions can be extreme, as well as contradictory! If we want to overcome the flaws of traditional approaches, we need to accept that this is a feature of the way we think.

The six elements and examples of the types of questions they prompt are as follows:

H = Helpful: "How helpful do I find what they are asking me to do?"

U = Understand: "Do I understand what they are asking me to do?" and "Do I understand why they are asking me to do it?"

M = Manageable: "How manageable is what they are asking me to do?"

A = Acceptable: "How acceptable do I find what they're asking me to do?" and "Do I accept that they have the authority to do so?" The more acceptable they find what we're asking them to do, the more likely they are to do it.

N = Normal: "Is what they are asking me to do, normal?" and "Are other people doing this?"

S = Salient:[3] "How relevant is what they are asking me to do?" and "How appealing is what they are asking me to do?"

Although the majority of questions sound simple, as we'll discover, there's more to them than we might initially think. You might also have noticed that although the entire framework is subjective, the later elements are a little more subjective than the earlier ones. For example, we will probably find it easier to identify whether our employees are likely to find something helpful than whether they find it salient.

Affordances

As well as using HUMANS to help us assess BIs, we can also use it to explore affordances. Affordances are a concept from design that describes potential alternative uses of objects.[4] In this case, we can think of affordances as alternatives to compliance; not what we would *like* people to do, but what they *could* do.

By using HUMANS to think about affordances, we can see how the alternatives to doing what we want stack up and therefore how tempting those might be, relative to our desired outcome. This allows us to play devil's advocate and see how they are likely to perceive the options of noncompliance or partial compliance.

What the HUMANS Framework Is Not

To get the most out of HUMANS, we need to understand its limitations. Knowing what it *isn't* and *can't* do will make us more aware of what it *is* and *can* do.

The framework is not a checklist that you can slavishly follow. It is a tool that you can use to identify dynamics that *might* be relevant to the outcome you are looking to achieve. In some cases, all elements will be helpful. In others, one or two might be all you need.

The individual elements in the framework are neither an exhaustive nor exclusive list of relevant factors you may want to consider. On many occasions, they will counteract each other; on others, they will work in unison to drive an extreme reaction.

The framework, in common with the entire Humanized Risk approach, excludes consideration of incentives and punishment.

The framework is not designed to be a model that weights each element and produces a score at the end. That's not to say you can't or shouldn't try to score them. By all means, please do so, but remember that the analysis you will be doing is qualitative and not quantitative. Any score is therefore highly subjective.

Notes

1. The reference to 44 pages comes from https://humanizingrules.link/dress

2. Eagle-eyed readers will note that these posters will serve little purpose, since anyone seeing them will, in theory, already be complying with the policy.

3. Salient comes from the Latin verb "salire" meaning "to leap". Nowadays it is used to describe things that "leap out", for example, when someone makes a "salient point" in an argument.

4. For example, an affordance for a chair, might be using it as a small ladder. While the designer clearly hasn't intended it for this purpose, it can easily be used in this way.

CHAPTER 10
H IS FOR HELPFUL

Der Grüne Pfeil

If you've ever driven in Germany and had to stop at a traffic light, you might have noticed a square sign to the right of the red light. The sign is known as the "grüne Pfeil" or green arrow and it's there to signal to drivers that they can "turn right on red" providing they stop to check it is safe to do so. While the vast majority of road signs are simply there to prohibit, mandate, warn, or inform us, the green arrow is far more driver-friendly.[1]

Not only does it give them the right to ignore another traffic regulation that could unnecessarily delay them, but it permits them to choose whether or not to exercise that right. I think that makes it one of the most helpful road signs I've ever come across and the perfect introduction to the first element of the HUMANS framework.

H Is for Helpful

The principle behind "Helpful" is that the more helpful our employees find what we are asking them to do, the more likely they are to do it. Conversely, the less helpful they think it is, the less likely they are to do it. A simple way to think about it is the concept of headwinds and tailwinds. Things that are helpful are like a tailwind propelling us towards our end goal; things that are unhelpful are like headwinds, that slow us down.

Since "Helpful" is the first element of the HUMANS framework, I will briefly explain the three main ways in which we can use it. The same principles apply to all of the later elements. The three ways that we can use "Helpful" are as follows:

1. The first is that we can explore the degree to which our employees will find what we are asking them to do, helpful or unhelpful. If we discover

that what we are asking them to do is unhelpful, then we may also wish to explore an additional area: how helpful or unhelpful *the idea* of what we are asking them to do is. The idea behind this is to try to establish whether the reason they find something unhelpful is a matter of principle, or whether it is the way in which we have implemented the request. We might, for example, have taken something that would ordinarily be viewed as helpful and made it feel unhelpful. In that case, there may be options to adjust the way in which we make the request of our employees.

2. The second is that we can identify ways in which we can make what we are asking our employees to do feel more or less helpful; in simple terms, how we frame the request. If we want to deter something, we can try to find ways to make it feel less helpful, if we want to encourage something, we can try to find ways to make it feel more helpful.

3. The third is that we can use it to explore how helpful they find the alternatives to what we have asked them to do. If our employees find noncompliance or partial compliance to be notably more helpful or unhelpful than compliance, then we can think about adjusting how we approach our request. For example, if not doing what we're asking our employees to do is seen by them as being significantly more helpful, we may need to make adjustments. Or, simply be aware of the fact when assessing the risk.

What Is Helpful?

We're all familiar with the word "helpful". We use it to describe explanations or actions that we feel have increased our knowledge, solved a problem, or been otherwise useful. If someone is helpful, they've said or done something that improves things from our perspective. To help us think about how our employees might perceive things and what we can do to shift their perception, here's a simple example.

Imagine we own a car dealership and we are going to ask our employees to log a report each time they interact with a potential customer. This will provide us with useful management information about how many potential customers we are speaking to and how effective those interactions are. From our perspective the reports are helpful. But will our employees think writing the report is helpful? On the face of it, the answer is likely to be "no". It will take time and either prevent them from speaking to potential customers, or require them to work longer hours in order to complete it.

So, how might we make it more helpful from their perspective? The answer is to make it worth the effort. I don't mean financially; just because you pay someone to do something doesn't make what you're asking them to do more helpful! It might make completing the reports more palatable, or even attractive – something we cover under "Salient" – but it wouldn't make them more helpful. Nor, by the way, does making the report easier to complete; that will make it more manageable, which is covered in the third element of the framework, but not more helpful.

The way we can make the report helpful is to think about what happens after it is filed. If it is merely entered into a contact database and they never hear about it again, then from the employee's perspective, that's not particularly helpful. Nor is using the data we gain from it to admonish the people filling it in; though, you could argue that if it is also used to encourage or reward good performers, then they may find it helpful! But those being admonished, won't. If, on the other hand, we provide them with insights – for example, sharing lessons learned on how to close sales more successfully – then they're getting something that will make the exercise feel more helpful.

As with all of the elements of the HUMANS framework, we also need to think about the alternatives available to them. It might seem more helpful from their perspective not to write reports and have more time to serve customers, or to fill in "tick box" reports that are useless, but technically compliant.

We'll come back to the car dealership reports when it is useful to do so for other elements. For the remainder of this chapter, I'm going to highlight a few of the dynamics that can make things more or less helpful from our employees' perspective.

Timing Is Everything

One of the key drivers as to whether something is helpful is timing. Get your timing right and something neutral can seem helpful; get it wrong, and something that might otherwise be helpful, can suddenly be rendered unhelpful.

We know this from our day-to-day lives. Those times when we're bombarded with ads for a product we were researching online, but have now bought, so no longer need; I don't know about you, Amazon, but I think one trampoline is more than enough! Signs warning us about roadworks that are going to disrupt our journey, that appear at a point when it is too late to find an alternative route. Or, simply when someone responds to a request with two simple words: "Not now."

Timing, as they say, is everything. An intervention that comes at a time when a decision has already been made is too late. Equally an intervention that comes too early will have less, if any, influence.

Key Questions

For each element of the framework, I will highlight some key questions that the element seeks to explore. These are not designed to be an exhaustive list of all the questions we might ask, but are there to help guide us as we explore each element. At the end of each chapter, there is a list of additional questions that are relevant to that framework.

Since we are looking to understand how our employees are likely to think and not how we would like them to think, the questions are all framed from that perspective. Although the questions are phrased in a binary manner, the answers they produce are more likely to be scalar in nature. The key questions which "Helpful" is seeking to answer are:

1a. Is what they are asking me to do helping or hindering me?

If the answer to 1a. is "hindering", then we might also wish to explore whether this is driven by the idea of what we are asking them to do, or the execution of it. In some circumstances, we might also wish to understand to what extent something our employees find helpful is because of the idea of it, as opposed to the way we have gone about it. In that case, 1b. would also be useful.

1b. Is the principle of what they are asking me to do helping or hindering me?

2. Is there an alternative to what they are asking me to do that would be more helpful?

3. Is this a good time for them to be asking?

4. What's in it for me?

Note

1. Readers interested in learning more about road signs may be interested in the Vienna Convention on Road Signs & Signals, a multinational treaty that seeks to standardise traffic regulations: https://humanizingrules.link/road

CHAPTER 11
U IS FOR UNDERSTAND

Save the Surprise

In 2012, the multi-award-winning film director Danny Boyle directed a performance unlike anything he'd directed before. As artistic director of the opening ceremony of the London Olympic Games, he was responsible for a live show costing £27 million that would be performed in front of 80,000 spectators in the stadium and billions of TV viewers worldwide. To ensure things ran as smoothly as possible on the night, Boyle invited 60,000 Olympic volunteers, prize-winners and other guests to a technical rehearsal, five days before the actual ceremony.

In order to maintain secrecy around the show's contents, Boyle spoke to the audience and asked them not to share photographs or details of the event on social media. Having told them they were the first people in the world to see the show, he asked for their help to "save the surprise" and the hashtag #SaveTheSurprise was displayed on screens in the stadium. Boyle crossed his fingers that nothing major would leak. It didn't. Rather than sharing details of the show, people shared their thoughts about it using the hashtag.

What Boyle had realised was the fact his audience would naturally want to talk about what they'd seen. By explaining *why* he needed them not to reveal details of the show and recognising that "save the surprise" would be more appealing than saying "keep the secret", Boyle persuaded the audience to willingly do what he wanted them to. Perhaps unsurprisingly, given he's a film director, Boyle had not only understood his audience, but he'd also ensured that they understood what he wanted.

U Is for Understood

The principles that underpinned #SaveTheSurprise are a perfect example of what "Understood", the second element of HUMANS, is all about. Before we explore further, it is worth noting that "Understood" should be read as meaning "comprehend" as opposed to "liking" or "agreeing to"; those nuances are covered by "Acceptable".

"Understood" is one of the more complex elements and explores three separate areas:

1. The first area is whether our employees understand *what* we want them to do. #SaveTheSurprise worked because the audience understood that they needed to not divulge details of the opening ceremony. If our employees don't comprehend what we are asking them to do, then there is a risk that they will either be incapable of complying, or only partially able to comply. In some cases, the need to understand is scalar – the more they understand, the more they are able to comply – while in others it is binary; you either understand and comply, or you do not. Of course, even if they don't comprehend, it is still theoretically possible in some cases, for them to be "unknowingly" or "accidentally" compliant; they don't understand what we are asking them to do, but they somehow manage to do it anyway.

2. The next area is whether our employees understand *why* we want them to do it. The #SaveTheSurprise audience understood the reason why they were being asked to do it and why that was important. If the rationale for the request hadn't been made clear to them, they might not have done. Explaining the "why" was necessary both to get the audience's buy-in and for practical reasons. This is particularly important for rules with qualitative components. As we will explore in more detail in Part III of this book, there are certain rules that require our employees not only to understand *what* we are asking them to do, but also *why*, so that they can comply to a certain standard. Sometimes, as with #SaveTheSurprise, there is simply a baseline of knowledge required, On other occasions, there is more of a linear correlation; the greater the level of comprehension, the greater the ability to comply.

3. The final area is the question of whether our employees think that *we* understand what we are asking them to do. In some respects, it isn't a question that obviously belongs in this section, since it is more relevant to elements like "Acceptable" or "Normal" which explore how our employees feel about the "reasonableness" of what we are asking them to do. However, since it covers similar ground to the other questions we are asking in this

chapter, I felt it was more appropriate to include it here. The idea behind it is that propensity to comply can in some instances be heavily influenced by the credibility of the person making the request. For the 2012 Olympics Opening Ceremony, Danny Boyle made it very clear to the dress rehearsal audience that he recognised the scale of what he was asking them to do. Not just in the way that he explained it to them. By providing the #SaveTheSurprise hashtag, the organisers showed the audience that they understood that they would want to share their experience with friends on social media, and gave them a frame for doing it, without revealing the contents.

The Curse of Dunning and Kruger

One of the challenges with the concept of understanding is that the shadow of Dunning and Kruger hangs over it (see Chapter 6). After all, our would-be heist hero McArthur Wheeler *thought* he understood how invisible ink worked, when clearly he did not! We've all seen examples of people knowing *what* they need to do, but failing to understand *why*. Just in case you haven't, there's an example of an embarrassing story of when it happened to me, in a couple of chapters' time!

We also need to be mindful of the curse of knowledge. If we need our employees to understand something, then we need to remember that what seems obvious to us might not to them. We know why we're implementing a particular rule; they might not. That doesn't mean that we need them to have our level of understanding; they just need to know enough for it to make sense to them.

It can be tempting to see the Dunning–Kruger Effect as an employee problem, and the curse of knowledge as our problem. However, it's worth remembering that we can also display Dunning–Krugeresque tendencies, by thinking we know more about life on the front line than we really do and therefore imposing requirements that don't make sense. Equally, employees can suffer from the curse of knowledge; not understanding that we don't have the experience that they have.

Before you worry that we're entering a cognitive circle of hell, there's a simple solution here. Since we're the ones who are seeking to impose rules on our employees, it's incumbent on us to solve this problem. In simple terms, that means spending time thinking about things from our employees' perspective and recognising that we, like them, can make flawed judgements.

Key Questions

To explore whether our employees are likely to find something more or less understandable, we need to consider the following questions; as ever, all are worded from the perspective of the employee:

1. Do I understand *what* they are asking me to do?
2. Do I understand *why* they are asking me to do it?
3. Do *they* understand what they are asking me to do?

CHAPTER 12
M IS FOR MANAGEABLE

See Something, Say Something

In 1984, a group of terrorists attempted to assassinate the UK Prime Minister Margaret Thatcher by bombing the hotel she was staying in. They failed, though tragically they did kill five other people. In a statement, the group said: "Today we were unlucky, but remember we only have to be lucky once. You will have to be lucky always." It's a sobering thought.

One of the ways the police have responded to this dynamic is to rely on members of the public to act as their eyes and ears. By asking them to report suspicious activities or things that look out of place, there's a greater chance of preventing bad outcomes. The challenge that poses is that the average member of the public isn't a security expert, so won't always be able to tell what is a genuine threat and what isn't. They may also not want to feel like they are wasting police time on something that could have an innocent explanation. Which is why many police forces have introduced mechanisms designed to address this.

In the UK, there's "See It. Say It. Sorted", a campaign that encourages members of the public to report things, no matter how insignificant, to a dedicated phone or text number. The word "sorted" is designed to provide a sense of closure; "if you report it to us, we'll take care of it" is the implied message. In the US, the equivalent of "See It. Say It. Sorted." is "See Something, Say Something". To support that, the authorities have also released "See Something, Send Something", an app that allows members of the public to send photographs or written notes of suspicious activities or items to the authorities.

By removing both psychological and logistical barriers to reporting, these campaigns make it easier for people to help the police. That in turn, should increase the number of reports and hopefully give them more of that all-important luck.

M Is for Manageable

"See It. Say It. Sorted" is a prime illustration of the first of two principles that under-pin "Manageable". By making things we want people to do easier, we make it more likely they will do them. Conversely, if there are things we don't want them to do, then making them harder will make it less likely that they will do them.

It is also worth being aware that if we can't make the thing we want them to do easier, then it may also be possible to make alternative options feel harder. To put it another way, if compliance can't be made easier, then we can also think about making non compliance harder.

Equally, we need to be mindful that it isn't the actual ease of doing something that matters. It is the perception of how hard it is that is critical. So, if we can't make something easier in reality, we may be able to make it *seem* easier. For example, by "chunking", breaking up a big task into lots of smaller tasks.

When a Fine Is a Fee

The second principle that Manageable explores is best explained via a story. A number of years ago I worked for someone who had a driver who would take him to and from work. On the odd occasion the driver was unavailable, he would drive himself. One day, I met him as he was coming getting out of his car. I noticed that he'd parked illegally. Not, I might add, in an inconsiderate way; there was no reason why it would inconvenience anyone else. However, since there were parking patrols in that area, I realised that if he planned to stay there all day, he'd likely get fined or have his car towed away.

I pointed this out to him and have never forgotten his response: "They can fine me, and take the car away and fine me for that as well, it's still cheaper than paying for parking and it's far more convenient." He had a point. If the car did get towed away, he'd just send his driver to collect it.

It's a great example of when a fine becomes a fee. Something that is supposed to act as a deterrent, actually incentivises the activity it is designed to prevent. There's a famous experiment conducted in an Israeli daycare centre where parents were fined if they were late in collecting their kids.[1]

When the fines were introduced, late collections increased. Far from deterring, the fine served to legitimise the action; you are paying to be allowed to do it, so you no longer feel guilty. As an aside, they removed the fine regime when they realised the impact, and although late collection rates declined, they never fell back to pre-fine levels.

The difference between the two stories is that the parents knew that there was a 100% chance that they would have to pay the fine if they were late. My former boss, on the other hand, was just playing "parking attendant roulette"; even if he lost the "game", he still was better off overall.

The "fine is a fee" stories help to introduce the second principle behind Manageable, which focuses on noncompliance. In doing so, it considers how our employees perceive both the likelihood and consequences of getting caught being noncompliant. The principle is as follows: the more "manageable" noncompliance is, the more likely they are not to comply.

In practice, employees for whom these factors are relevant are likely to consider both together. In some environments, the likelihood of getting caught could be more of a significant factor than the consequences.

Key Questions

To explore whether our employees are likely to find something more or less manageable, we need to consider the following questions; as ever, all are worded from the perspective of the employee.

1a. Is what they are asking me to do manageable?
    If the answer to 1a. is "no", then we might also wish to ask:

1b. Is the idea of what they are asking me to do manageable?

2. Is there an alternative option available to me that I would find more manageable?

3. Am I deterred by the consequences of noncompliance with what I am being asked to do?

4. Do I think I am likely to be caught if I am noncompliant?

Note

1. Uri Gneezy and Aldo Rustichini, "A Fine Is a Price", *Journal of Legal Studies*, 29(1) (1970): 1–17. doi:10.1086/468061.

CHAPTER 13
A IS FOR ACCEPTABLE

Rebalancing the Marketplace

If you've ever tried to book an Uber at a busy time like a Friday night or New Year's Eve, and found yourself being quoted an exorbitant price for your fare, you've encountered something called "surge pricing". Commonly used by ride-sharing companies, the principle behind models like "surge pricing" is based on a simple economic model: if the demand for rides exceeds the supply of drivers, an algorithm increases the price. As Uber explains on their website, this approach "encourages more drivers to serve a busy area over time and shifts rider demand, to maintain reliability and restore balance".

While economists and ride share drivers love surge pricing, passengers tend not to. After all, the reason we're hailing a ride is because we have an immediate need to get from A to B. Being asked to pay a higher than normal price for that – often a multiple of the normal price – can feel like you're being ripped off. Particularly when the price can fluctuate wildly within a short period of time. Context plays a big part here. We instinctively know that airlines and hotels also put prices up when there is a lot of demand, but we tend not to be booking those at the last minute, so it usually feels less egregious.

Context also explains another reason why passengers often dislike surge pricing. The algorithms that manage it don't – because they can't – make any distinction between increased demand as a result of rain or increased demand because people are fleeing from a terrorist incident. We might accept the former, but the latter feels unethical and highly exploitative. To solve this, Uber has instituted manual reviews of instances where surge pricing has unexpectedly kicked in; if the reason is something that would make the company look bad, they immediately override the algorithm and suspend it.

A Is for Acceptable

Just as we can think of surge pricing in terms of whether we might or might not find it acceptable, the third element of the framework asks the same question about our rules.

The principle behind "Acceptable" is that the more acceptable our employees find what we are asking them, the more likely they are to do it. Conversely, the less acceptable they find it, the less likely they are to do it.

The element explores the acceptability of two different components. The first is the rule itself, and the second is the authority that we have to request they comply with it. We'll return to the latter in Chapter 23.

Is It Fair?

One of the key dynamics behind "Acceptable" is a sense of fairness. If we think something is unfair, we are less likely to respect it. And when it comes to things that are unfair, a common dynamic called Sludge is right up there!

In the introduction to BeSci, I explained the concept of "Nudge": the idea that we can change the choice architecture to influence people's choices. Now meet Nudge's evil cousin, "Sludge". It's a term coined by *Nudge* author Richard Thaler to describe something that deliberately makes choices harder. If, like me recently, you've tried to cancel a subscription and had to jump through a ridiculous number of hoops to do so, you'll be very familiar with it.

In my case, it was the *Wall Street Journal* who had offered me an introductory discount, and made it incredibly easy for me to take out a subscription. But when that rate doubled, I couldn't justify paying it, so I tried to cancel. Not only could I not do that online, but I had to call during office hours to speak to someone. Entirely predictably, their entire focus was on trying to dissuade me from cancelling; ironically, they even offered to reinstate the introductory rate! Since I had absolutely no faith that I wouldn't end up back in the same place in a year's time, I declined. In part, as a matter of principle.

The practice of inserting Sludge into processes is so pernicious and commonplace, that Germany has introduced a law that requires companies to allow customers to cancel subscriptions within two clicks on their website.[1] After all, if you can make it easy for people to sign up online, you should also be able to make it just as easy to cancel.

How Do We Know Something Is Fair?

While fairness is obviously a highly subjective measure – what seems fair to me, might not to you – research has identified some common factors that apply when it comes to rules. In his book, *Outcome-Based Cooperation*,[2] Professor Christopher Hodges summarises the five main factors that affect whether people will obey rules:

a. The rules are made through a fair *process*; where people feel that they have had involvement, or a possibility for voice and input.

b. The *substance* of the rule is perceived to be fair by the individual and most of the community, even if individuals do not agree with it.

c. The rule accords with their sense of *values*; namely the values of the individual, the particular community or social group or organisation.

d. The rule is *applied* fairly by/to all.

e. Most people are *observing* the rule.

Note how often the word "fair" appears in the list!

Key Questions

To explore whether our employees are likely to find something more or less acceptable, we need to consider the following questions; as ever, all are worded from the perspective of the employee.

1a. Is the rule they are asking me to comply with acceptable?
      If the answer to 1a. is "no", then we might also wish to ask:

1b. Is the idea of what they are asking me to do acceptable?

2. Do I accept that they have the authority to impose this rule?

3. Is what the rule is trying to achieve fair?

4. Is the rule consistent with the values of the organisation?

5. Is it fairly applied to all employees; particularly those who are setting the rules?

Notes

1. *Gesetz für Faire Verbraucherverträge*, published in the Federal Gazette (Part I) no. 53/2021, p. 3433 et seq., full text publicly available (in German) at: https://humanizingrules.link/cancel.

2. Christopher Hodges, *Outcome-Based Cooperation: In Communities, Business, Regulation, and Dispute Resolution* (London: Bloomsbury, 2022).

CHAPTER 14
N IS FOR NORMAL

You Don't Need a Label

As a frequent train traveller between London and Munich, I'm a member of several train travel–related groups on Facebook. They're a rare example of where social media really is a force for good. Usually I'm learning travel tips from other people, but occasionally I'm able to help others. Like a lady who was travelling for the first time on the Eurostar service between London and Brussels. She had a question: "The website says you have to put a label on your luggage with your name, destination and seat number on it, but where do I get hold of a label?"

Flush with pride at the fact there was a question I actually knew the answer to, I responded with a Dunning and Kruger level of confidence. "I wouldn't worry about it", I wrote, "In theory, you need one, but in practice you honestly don't." I knew I was right, because I had lots of evidence to prove it.

Not only had I never used a label, but I'd never seen anyone else use one. Except, that is, people with oversized or unusual luggage like musical instruments or bird cages. But then, that's normal on trains when you're taking something like that, just in case it goes missing or they ask you to store it somewhere else. I'd also never seen a member of Eurostar staff check whether bags were labelled, either at the stations or on trains. In any case, I had no idea where you'd get hold of one of their labels anyway. Thrilled that I'd been able to show off my frequent traveller knowledge, I considered the matter closed.

Until a Eurostar employee replied with something that (pun intended) stopped me in my tracks. He pointed something out that hadn't occurred to me. If, he explained, there is an emergency evacuation, then you're not allowed to take your luggage with you for safety reasons. Without a label, there's a big risk that Eurostar won't be able to identify whose bag it is. Best case, you don't get your bag back for a long time, worst case you don't get it back at all.

Suddenly, I felt rather foolish. Because when you think about it, this makes perfect sense. I realised that because that's not something you normally have to do when you catch other trains, I'd assumed it was a silly rule. But most trains don't travel through the longest undersea tunnel in the world.[1] Evacuations don't happen that often, but they do occur and I'm a fairly frequent traveller on the route. Since then, I've always put labels on my bags whenever I travel on Eurostar.

However, my idiocy does at least serve a purpose by allowing me to introduce the fifth element of the framework. I didn't think putting labels on my bags was "Normal", so I didn't do it.

N Is for Normal

It is this principle of what is "Normal" which drives the fifth element of the framework. The more "Normal" our employees think what we are asking them to do is, the more likely they are to do it. Conversely, the less "Normal" they think it is, the less likely they are to do it.

There are two different nuances of "Normal" that we need to consider. The first is what we might term "standard", in the sense of Standard Operating Procedure; whether our employees think what we're asking them to do is something they would ordinarily expect to be asked to do, in that type of situation. It's the employee equivalent of my belief that since it isn't normal to put labels on bags on trains, I didn't think I should have to on Eurostar.

The second relates to "social", in the sense of social norms; whether our employees think that what we are asking them to do is something other people would do. We can see this in my response to the label issue, where my perspective was, in part, influenced by the fact I hadn't ever seen anyone else use one.

The reason for drawing a distinction between "standard practices" and "social norms" is that this will allow us to understand any potential impediments to achieving our desired outcome. We might, for example, be seeking to introduce a process that is perfectly normal within the industry we're in, but the way in which we've done it, isn't. That tells us that – all other things being equal – we stand a good chance of being able to implement the process, but we may need to adjust our approach.

Key Questions

To explore whether our employees are likely to find something more or less normal, we need to consider the following questions; as ever, all are worded from the perspective of the employee.

1. Is *what* they are asking me to do normal?
   If the answer to 1a. is "no", then we might also wish to ask:

1b. Is it normal to be asked to comply with this type of rule?

2. Is complying with this rule something other people would normally do?

3. Are other people complying with this rule?

4. Do I feel particularly drawn towards either the group that is compliant or the group that is noncompliant?

Note

1. https://humanizingrules.link/tunnel

CHAPTER 15
S IS FOR SALIENT

I Thought It Would Be Bigger

If you've ever been to Paris, you've probably been to the Louvre Museum. Pick a random "top ten things to do in Paris" list, and it'll be there somewhere, along with the Eiffel Tower. And I'm willing to bet that if you've been to the Louvre, you'll also have seen the most famous painting in the museum, the Mona Lisa by Leonardo da Vinci.

I've been to the Louvre more times than I can remember – full disclosure: I used to live in Paris – but I've only seen the Mona Lisa once. Like many other famous "must sees" like the Manneken Pis in Brussels or the Little Mermaid in Copenhagen, it's not something I ever need to see again. Not because it's a bad painting, but because, like the two statues, the reality is a bit disappointing, relative to what I'd expected. So many other things in the Louvre are far more impressive. Yet, if you ever told anyone you'd been to the Louvre and not seen the Mona Lisa, they'd look at you in a strange way, as if to suggest the entry fee had been a complete waste of money.

Which is why, if you haven't yet been, do the touristy thing and see it. And then have a look around you.[1] You'll notice that hardly anyone is paying attention to anything else in the same gallery. Even though there are some stunning pieces of art on display there. Notice how I didn't even bother trying to dissuade you from seeing it. I just accepted that you would. Even though I've told you it's incredibly disappointing, you're going to want to go and see it for yourself.

On any objective level, that makes absolutely no sense whatsoever. Not that you're ignoring my advice, but that we all feel obliged to see it. But intuitively, we all understand why. Because it's famous, it grabs our attention over anything else. Incidentally, if you want to know why it's famous and what that has to do with

Pablo Picasso, then I highly recommend reading *You're Invited* by Jon Levy,[2] where he reveals the entire story.

What we're experiencing with the Mona Lisa is something known as salience. When something is "Salient", it means it is emotionally or physically striking in a way that grabs our attention over other things. Saliency typically arises from the contrast between items and their surrounding environment. That might be a brightly coloured coat against a grey background, or the number 12 in the following sequence: A D E 12 C R W.

S Is for Salient

"Salient" is the most complex of all the elements, which is why it comes last. The principle behind it is that the more salient our employees find what we are asking them to do, the more they will pay attention to it. Conversely, the less salient they find it, the less they will pay attention to it.

Since we only have limited energy capacity, we tend to deploy it on things we deem worthy of our attention. As we saw when we explored the concept of repetition suppression, this is highly subjective. We will pay more attention to things we've never seen before or things that seem unusual, over things we have seen before or seem usual.

Unlike the other elements in HUMANS, "Salient" is not exploring the likelihood of our employees doing what we are asking them to. Rather, it explores the likelihood of us having grabbed their attention. That can be good if we've done it in a positive way, or bad if we've done it in a negative way. Of course, just because we have their attention doesn't mean they'll do what we want them to. But, equally, if we don't get their attention, they won't know what it is we want them to do!

Since salience covers a broad range of dynamics, I thought I'd provide three simple examples of everyday attempts to make things more salient.

Coffee Shop

The first example comes courtesy of coffee chain Starbucks who use personalisation to make something relatively ordinary feel more salient. It happens when they ask you for your name when ordering coffee. By asking customers for their name when they order, they're making the experience more personal.

It not only makes it easier to collect drinks – shouting "cappuccino" when you've got lots of people waiting for one is unhelpful – but it is also designed to make people feel like the coffee has been made specially for them. At least, that's what they tell us.

And those occasions when they misspell a name? It's a feature not a bug. In a noisy environment, under time pressure and with different ways you can spell names, let alone the fact there are some names the staff might be unfamiliar with, it is going to happen. Not to mention mischievous baristas who might intentionally mishear and customers who might fancy a name change. When it does, customers will definitely notice and many of them will share it on social media. That's not something you would do, if they got your name right.

Station Announcements

Making things unusual or fun is another way of making them salient and thereby grabbing our attention. In 2018, staff at London's Victoria Station noticed that passengers weren't always listening to important safety messages. So they decided to try something different and two members of staff asked their daughter to record announcements for them. Their idea was that the unusual sound of a child's voice would mean people paid more attention. They were right. Accidents on the escalators reduced by two-thirds after the announcements were introduced.

During the pre-Christmas period in 2021, they tried a different voice as part of a sponsored promotion. Singer Mariah Carey – famous for her multimillion selling song "All I Want for Christmas Is You" – asked festive revellers to take care on their way home. They didn't release any information on whether Mariah helped or hindered safety, but she certainly made it more salient.

Weather Forecasts

If like me, you find yourself watching weather forecasts, only to find you've not really paid much attention to what you saw, then there may be a good reason for it. In my case, it's obviously because I'm getting older and have a ridiculously short attention span. In your case, it might be because you're being presented with a lot of information that is sometimes hard to compute.

Usually, we watch a weather forecast for a particular reason. Most often to know which clothes we need to wear, but people with hobbies or jobs that are weather-dependent will have other reasons. Yet very often the forecast is often overly technical or general in nature. I've lost count of the number of times I've been given a forecast for a big city like London and then gone out, only to discover that there are ten different microclimates I'm going to experience in just a small part of that city. As a result, I tend to pay little attention to the weather forecasts.

Very often, this isn't helped by the fact the weather is presented in terms that make very little sense to me. I can barely cope with temperatures that are presented to me in Celsius, let alone when I see a US forecast in Fahrenheit. So I was delighted to come across something called the "Trash Can Wind Meter",[3] which is used to make wind strength more salient to TV viewers. It does this by using a scale that doesn't require you to be a weather expert. Rather than using "wind force" numbers, the different categories are:

- Lid flipped open.
- Tipped over.
- In the neighbour's yard.
- Down the street.
- I've lost my trash can.

It's salient, because it's very easy to understand, highly actionable, and memorable.

Key Questions

To explore whether our employees are likely to find something more or less salient, we need to consider the following questions; as ever, all are worded from the perspective of the employee.

1. Am I aware of what they are asking me to do?
2. How relevant is what they are asking me to do?
3. How curious/entertained/excited am I about what they are asking me to do?
4. How appealing is what they are asking me to do vs. doing the opposite?

Notes

1. Alternatively, if you're not going to be in Paris any time soon, do an images search, and you'll see what I mean.

2. Jon Levy, *You're Invited: The Art and Science of Connection, Trust and Belonging* (New York: Harper Business, 2021).

3. The one I originally saw was from the wonderfully named Channel 12 – The Weather Authority.

CHAPTER 16
HOW TO USE HUMANS

One of the benefits of HUMANS is that we can use it in several ways. In common with many other BeSci frameworks – some of which are listed at the end of this part of the book – there isn't a strict methodology that you need to follow to gain potentially valuable insights from it. This is deliberate. As we'll see in Part IV, where we'll explore behavioural data and the human biases associated with gathering and interpreting it, the quality and quantity of insights available can vary substantially.

For that reason, HUMANS is designed to be both a basic, high-level indicative guide or to do more sophisticated analysis. In its most straightforward application, you can quickly go through the individual elements of the framework and see if anything stands out. In my experience using the framework with clients, there are often just one or two factors that resonate far more than others, particularly when diagnosing why existing interventions aren't working as intended. If that's the case, you can just focus on those.

Alternatively, you could use it to do a more detailed analysis. Since the elements of HUMAN are scalar – in other words, the "answers" it produces, sit within a range – we can think about scoring the individual elements. Taking "Helpful" as an example, we can see that potential responses could sit on a scale from "Incredibly Unhelpful" to "Extremely Helpful". We might then choose to use scores between −20 for the former and +20 for the latter, like this:

Incredibly Unhelpful	Some-what Unhelpful	Unhelpful	Neutral	Helpful	Some-what Helpful	Extremely Helpful
−20	−10	−5	0	+5	+10	+20

The appeal of adding a score is that it allows us to rank the different elements and compare behavioural interventions with each other. For that reason, a few of my clients have opted to use HUMANS this way. Most of them have done so by directly asking a sample of their employees to provide the scores. If that appeals to you, then, by all means, go ahead, but be aware that you'll need to consider calibrating the different elements; for example, is "Extremely Helpful" worth as many points as "Incredibly Acceptable"?

The other thing to consider is that, in reality, a particular intervention might not produce as clear an answer as the scale might suggest. Our employees can perceive something as simultaneously "helpful" in some regards and "unhelpful" in others. While you could theoretically net the two off and conclude the intervention is "neutral", that potentially means missing some opportunities to create more creative interventions that maximise the high-scoring aspects and minimise the low-scoring ones.

Potential Actions

Whether reviewing an existing behavioural intervention or planning a new one, HUMANS can help inform our decision. Once we've analysed the actual or expected impact of a particular intervention, we can take one of several courses of action:

1. *Reject*: we opt not to continue with or implement the intervention. Either because – in extreme cases – we recognise that the "bad will" it generates exceeds the benefits of introducing it, or because it is unlikely to work in the way we had envisaged.

2. *Redesign*: we change the nature of the intervention to take account of the behavioural dynamics we have identified.

3. *Reframe*: we keep the substance of the intervention as it is but focus on reframing our employees' perception of it.

4. *Roll out regardless*: we continue with the intervention but recognise a greater risk of noncompliance and increase our monitoring and deterrence activities.

Standing on the Shoulders

Before we leave HUMANS, I want to highlight two additional BeSci frameworks – on whose shoulders I am standing – that you might also find helpful.

Both have helped to inspire some of the thinking behind HUMANS and my work with clients. Both can help you to humanize your rules.

Going Dutch

One of the pleasures of working in BeSci is that it is an international discipline. I work with colleagues across the globe. Some countries, like the Netherlands, are centres of excellence. The Dutch have a long history of deploying BeSci in exciting ways.

You'll find one of the most commonly replicated and cited BeSci interventions at Amsterdam's Schiphol airport. Sadly, it's only visible to half of you since it's in the men's toilets. Those unable to visit either the airport or the men's toilets can do an image search for what I'm about to describe. The idea of the intervention is to help gentlemen – how can I put this? – aim more accurately by providing a visible target. In this case, the image of a fly has been etched into the inside of the urinal.

While you're in the airport, do also look out for two other pieces of BeSci brilliance; though honestly, you won't be able to miss them! The first is "Real Time", a clock by Dutch artist Maarten Baas. It's a film of a man in blue overalls who paints the time, minute by minute. It's both eye-catching and unusual, making it highly salient for passengers, giving them no excuse to be late to the gate! The second is the iconic way-finding signage that makes navigating the terminals incredibly easy. It's a wonderful example. Designed by visual information designer Paul Mijksenaar, it's so much of a national icon that you'll find it in the Rijksmuseum, their national museum. Both the clock and the signage score highly on HUMANS!

On that basis, perhaps it's not surprising that the Netherlands have also come up with a groundbreaking BeSci framework that was one of the inspirations for HUMANS. I discovered it thanks to my friend and fellow behavioural traveller Roger Miles, who highlighted it in his *Conduct Risk Management*[1] book. It's called "The Table Of Eleven (TTOE)".[2]

TTOE was published in 1994 by the wonderfully named Law Enforcement Expertise Centre of the Dutch Ministry of Justice in The Hague. The very forward-thinking idea behind TTOE was to ensure that legislators should assess any proposed new laws for what I refer to as "compliability", in other words, how feasible and likely it is that people will comply with them.

TTOE assesses laws against two sets of criteria. First, intrinsic motivation to comply with the law, i.e., what would people's reactions to the concept be if there were no law governing it? Second, extrinsic motivation to comply with the law, i.e., how likely it is that people will get caught if they break the law.

Since HUMANS does not focus on enforcement measures such as reporting, inspection, and sanctions, readers interested in these topics will find TTOE well worth their time.

FEAST

The second framework comes from the Behavioural Insights Team (BIT), the original "Nudge Unit" I referred to in Chapter 5 on BeSci. Having originally published a comprehensive framework of behavioural drivers called MINDSPACE[3] – which may be of interest to readers looking for a more academic analysis – they also published a simpler, more user-friendly version called EAST.

EAST is short for Easy, Attractive, Social, and Timely and covers four basic principles that can support behavioural interventions. Readers interested in understanding where these elements fit into HUMANS will find "Easy" in "Manageable", "Attractive" in "Salient", "Social" in "Normal", and "Timely" in "Helpful".

When I usually teach EAST to my clients, I add an "F" to form FEAST. The "F" stands for "Fair" and reflects the importance of Rule Number Six; just because we can do a behavioural intervention doesn't mean we should. It also allows me to say that all my behavioural interventions begin with the concept of "Fairness". As an alternative, Professor Richard Thaler, co-author of *Nudge*,[4] has developed his version of FEAST where "F" stands for "Fun". When it comes to HUMANS, you'll find "Fairness" in "Acceptable" and "Fun" in "Salient".

While HUMANS is a more comprehensive framework, (F)EAST can provide an excellent entry point for those new to BeSci or who need a tool that they can very quickly deploy.

Other Frameworks Are Available

At this point, I need to highlight that having specifically referenced TTOE and EAST that – in the spirit of the disclaimer regularly deployed by the BBC – "other BeSci frameworks are available". Since no single framework can do justice to all relevant biases, heuristics, and dynamics, a compromise will always be required. For that reason, I tend to work with a number of them. Though, obviously, I start with – what else? – HUMANS.

Notes

1. Roger Miles, *Conduct Risk Management* (London: Kogan Page, 2017)

2. https://humanizingrules.link/ttoe

3. https://humanizingrules.link/mindspace

4. Richard H. Thaler and Cass R. Sunstein, *Nudge* (New York: Penguin, 2009)

PART III
THE SIX RULES

THE SIX RULES

CHAPTER 17
THE SIX RULES

Introduction

Since this book's title contains the word Rules, I thought we should have some. In each of the following six chapters, I will introduce you to a rule. Keeping with the book's spirit, they are not intended to be slavishly followed.

The rules are simply a means of highlighting common misconceptions about how we can best influence our employees. We can avoid making unnecessary mistakes and identify creative alternatives to solving our compliance challenges by being aware of them.

Rule One: Compliance Is an Outcome, Not a Process

In the same way that we rely on biases and heuristics to guide our thinking, we tend to lean on "tried and tested" processes when delivering compliance outcomes. Rule Number One encourages us to take a step back and think about what outcome we want to achieve. That way, we can choose the right tool for the job.

Rule Two: 100% Compliance Is Neither Achievable Nor Desirable

We often hear the phrase "zero tolerance" in relation to particular rules or requirements. While that sounds sensible, it isn't always realistic. In some cases, it can even be counter-productive. Rule Number Two highlights why and encourages us to think carefully about what outcome we actually need.

Rule Three: When Putting on a Show, Make Sure You Know Your Audiences

Very often, when trying to persuade people to behave in a particular manner, we do things for effect. That might mean showing a regulator how seriously we're taking their rules or making a control highly visible to deter wrongdoers. Rule Number Three encourages us to think about who our audiences are, what messages we might want to send them, and how we can avoid inadvertently sending unhelpful messages to unintended audiences.

Rule Four: Design for the Willing, Not the Wilful

When writing rules, we tend to think about the "bad" outcomes we're trying to prevent, and the "bad" people were trying to deter. That means we're not thinking about the vast majority of people who want to do the right thing. Rule Number Four encourages us to focus our efforts on them.

Rule Five: If One Person Breaks a Rule, You've Got a People Problem; If Lots of People Break a Rule, You've Got a Rule Problem

When people break a rule within an organisation, we rightly hold them accountable. But if many people are breaking that same rule, then it's unlikely they're all deliberately setting out to do so. It's more likely that the rule has something about it that is driving noncompliance. Rule Number Five helps us to think about why and what we can do about it.

Rule Six: Just Because You Can Doesn't Mean You Should

When deciding on a course of action or explaining it in hindsight, we can often turn to whether it is legal or otherwise permitted to justify what we do or have done. This applies to us as rule-setters. We can legally require many things of our employees, but is it correct or practical for us to always do so? It also applies to our employees. There are lots of things they are permitted or able to do. But should they? Rule Number Six explores these dynamics and how we can think about mitigating them.

CHAPTER 18
RULE NUMBER ONE

Beatings Will Continue Until Morale Improves

In 1789, a famous mutiny occurred on the *HMS Bounty*, a British Royal Navy vessel. A band of sailors led by acting-Lieutenant Fletcher Christian seized control of the ship from Captain William Bligh, who was set adrift with eighteen of his loyal crew. The story has been made into a musical, several movies, and countless books.

A common feature of the story's fictionalised versions is an order Bligh is said to have given to his men. Apparently, he told them, "Beatings will continue until morale improves." There is no evidence that Bligh actually said this. Nor is there any evidence that he also said, "Never let the truth stand in the way of a good anecdote."

As a memorable quote and "last straw" plot device to explain a mutiny, "beatings will continue" works really well. As an actual order, it makes no sense whatsoever. Administering beatings will not achieve the desired outcome of improved morale.

Outcome

What the fictional Bligh failed to understand was that engaging human beings isn't a matter of mandating or forcing it. As anyone who has experienced a corporate awayday with an element of "enforced fun" will appreciate, we can't force people to feel a particular way; they either do or they don't.

Of course, they can *pretend* to be having fun. Just as they can *pretend* to be following rules. But since we're interested in people *actually* doing what we want them to and not just going through the motions – particularly when no one is watching – we need to understand the underlying drivers. This is where Rule Number One comes in:

Compliance is an outcome, not a process.

As we saw in earlier chapters, it is easy to confuse the process we use to deliver a desired organisational outcome with that outcome. To put it another way, we mustn't confuse the "job" with the "tool" we use.

compliance Is Not Compliance

Since I'm going to use the "c" word a lot in these rules – "compliance", that is! – it's probably worth me reiterating what I explained in the definitions in an earlier chapter. Not for you, obviously, but for those readers who might have somehow managed to miss those pages!

When I refer to "small c" compliance in this book, I'm not talking about big "c" Compliance, the function. What I mean by "small c" compliance is an outcome: getting our employees to do what we want. That outcome might be to comply with a policy, or it might be to do something that has absolutely nothing to do with regulation, such as responding to an employee survey or using the office stairs as opposed to the elevator.

As someone who has worked in "big C" Compliance, it might surprise you to learn that I think the word is awful. It's one of the worst pieces of branding ever! If you wanted to signal that you were dull, bureaucratic, and officious, you'd choose a word like Compliance. And then you'd add the suffix "Officer". It's probably the only time the word "officer" makes something sound worse! That's not a criticism of the function, by the way, it's the branding I can't stand.

The reason I need to explain the difference between Compliance and compliance isn't just to avoid confusing you. It goes to the heart of this rule. This means I can write one of the most confusing sentences ever: While Compliance is a process, compliance is an outcome.

Look Where You Want to Go

If like me, you ride motorbikes, then you'll be familiar with a very simple rule. You learn it early in your riding career, ideally by being taught it rather than from experience! If you're riding around a bend, then the one thing you shouldn't do is look at the bend. Instead, you need to look where you want to go. Otherwise, you risk crashing into the thing you're fixating on avoiding. It's counter-intuitive, but as I can attest from personal experience, highly effective.

Yet, when it comes to compliance, we tend to do the opposite. Rather than thinking about the outcome we're looking to achieve, we focus more on the frameworks, processes, and policies we've implemented to get us there. This feels logical, and there are valid reasons why this happens. However, as we'll see, if we don't look at the outcome, we will rely on processes that won't always do what we want. In motorcycling terms, we're looking at the bend, not where we want to go.

The Business of Influencing Human Decision-Making

We tend to focus on process when we think about compliance because we understandably look at the challenge through an organisational lens. Since we aim to have the organisation be compliant, the logical solution is to have a Compliance function that ensures that can happen. They use frameworks, controls, policies, and rules to meet that objective.

However, organisations cannot be compliant of their own accord. You can't tell a brand, building, or legal entity what to do and expect a coherent response. The employees within the organisation will determine whether or not the organisation is compliant. The business of Compliance is, therefore, to influence human decision-making of the people within the organisation. If they succeed in that mission, the organisation is compliant. If they don't, it isn't.

Yet, more often than not, that isn't how Compliance functions are positioned or perceived. Ask the average employee what comes to mind when they hear the word "Compliance", and you're unlikely to get an enthusiastic response. If you're lucky, they'll say something about "rules" or "regulations". If you're unlucky, you'll get "business prevention unit". If you're really unfortunate, it'll be something I can't print in this book. You're unlikely to hear a word like "human".

I'm not suggesting that they need to win a popularity contest. Still, if we genuinely want to ensure that an organisation is compliant, we must ensure that Compliance has the mandate, skills, and resources to influence employee decision-making. Historically, most organisations haven't adopted that approach, which has meant that the processes designed to deliver compliance aren't thinking about influencing people.

The Human Algorithm Is Not Logical

As we saw from the traditional toolkit and the "beatings will continue" story, we often implicitly assume a linear relationship between the process we've put in place and the outcome we're looking to achieve. That makes perfect sense in environments with predictable dynamics. Suppose we're designing engineering processes that rely on the laws of Newtonian physics. Those laws will always apply in that case, and we know that following the procedure will deliver the outcome we're looking for.

Yet, as we've seen in the earlier chapters, human decision-making isn't logical. If, for example, we write something in a policy, we might logically expect our employees to read, understand, and comply with it. But, in reality, we know that might not happen for various reasons. People can be forgetful, negligent, in a hurry, or any number of other things that can mean they don't always do logical things. That's before we think about people being creative in terms of how they interpret rules. Equally, people writing rules don't always get them right. They're fallible and miss things as much as the people for whom they write the rules.

We also need to remember a simple fact. The average employee isn't interested in Compliance. If they were, they'd be working in the Compliance function. What they are interested in is compliance. Most people want to turn up to work and do a good job, not break any rules, and do the right thing. The role of Compliance is, therefore, to help them achieve that. For that to happen requires us to humanize our rules.

CHAPTER 19
RULE NUMBER TWO

Zero Accidents

During a visit to Hong Kong, I spotted a sign that grabbed my attention. It read "Zero Accidents on the Road, Hong Kong's Goal". Next to that was an appealing logo of an anthropomorphised egg, complete with eyes, arms, and legs with a road wrapped around it. The logo, I later discovered, is called "Mr Safegg". The egg shape represents "zero" while the road wrapped around the egg is in the shape of an S which is short for "safety".

The sign was put there by the Hong Kong Safety Council (HKSC), who are behind the noble mission it promotes. It's an excellent idea, in theory. After all, who wouldn't want to have accident-free roads? Answer: anyone who makes money from accidents, but let's move on. While most of us would like to have entirely safe roads, we also know that it's pretty unrealistic. At least for as long as you have humans driving vehicles.

Zero Tolerance

Many organisations adopt a similar approach when it comes to compliance and ethics. How often have you heard phrases like "we have zero tolerance for X"? It's so commonplace that it's almost a cliché.

As with Mr Safegg, it's nice to have something to aspire to. But if it's actually unachievable, then does it really make sense? And might there be a downside? This is where Rule Number Two comes in:

> 100% compliance is neither achievable nor desirable.

If you think that sounds outrageous, let me explain. I'm not saying you should allow people to do what they want. Nor am I saying that every single rule or requirement should be subject to a degree of tolerance. When I say "100%

compliance", I mean in aggregate. There will be specific rules where we do need 100% compliance. Or, as close as we can get to 100%. But there are others we really don't, or it's just not feasible.

So, 100% compliance is an impossible dream because the people you're trying to influence aren't entirely reliable. That's not a criticism; it just means they're human.

People Are People

Much as you might like this not to be the case, the people you're trying to influence are fallible. Not because you've hired terrible people, but because they're human. As we saw when we explored the basics of BeSci, the human algorithm isn't perfect. Every single one of us – even you, dear reader – makes mistakes, breaks laws, circumvents rules, and tells lies. Not all of the time, of course. More often than not, we won't do those things. But sometimes –probably more often than we might like to admit – we will.

Brian Cullinan is a prime illustration that even the best-intentioned people with lots of experience can and do make mistakes (see the Introduction). Indeed, it is often their experience that blinds them. There's a paradox that comes with being in a senior position. On the one hand, junior or inexperienced people will make mistakes because of their lack of experience. Yet the very experience we think is lacking in junior people can blind senior people and cause them also to make mistakes.

Writing rules for Mr Logic, the cartoon character I referred to in Chapter 5, is easy because he'll respond in an entirely predictable, rational manner. Writing rules for ordinary people is much more challenging because we evolve and learn from experience. What we feel about something today might be very different to how we feel about it in a year. Unlike Mr Logic, we'll have a human response to what we're told to do.

The World Is Changing

We're also not operating in a static or stable environment. This means that when it comes to solving problems or delivering business success, there may not be a helpful precedent or "playbook" answer to which we can quickly turn. In many cases, trade-offs will be necessary. The "right" answer may demand that people override conventional wisdom or break the rules. History is littered with famous names like Sir Isaac Newton, Galileo Galilei, and Rosa Parks, whose undeniable contributions to progress saw them do precisely that.

The fact that we're dealing with sentient, fallible beings operating in a changing environment poses a huge challenge to people who need to write or enforce rules. Even the best rules writer will likely struggle to predict how people might react to their rules and the circumstances in which those rules might be applied. A rule designed for an analogue world might not work in a digital one.

So, if 100% compliance is impossible to achieve, what can we do about it? The good news is that sometimes we don't necessarily need to do anything. In fact, a certain level of noncompliance might actually be desirable.

Hiring Humans to Be Human

Counter-intuitively, the reasons we hire people in the twenty-first century, particularly in the Knowledge Economy, may make them less compliant. As technology evolves, what we ask people to do in the workplace is changing. Tasks that are repetitive and predictable can be given to machines, which are cheaper, better at them than we are, and don't need health care or holidays.

That means we're hiring people to do the things the machines can't (yet), tasks that involve skills like nuance, judgement, and emotional intelligence. While these skills bring out the best in humans, they can also bring out the worst. They're also often the skills that help and encourage people to challenge, bend, or break the rules.

Hiring people to be creative or disruptive means they may also apply that creativity and disruptiveness to the rules they're being asked to comply with. Telling them that we expect 100% compliance if that's genuinely impossible risks us losing credibility. If we're hiring smart people, we can expect them to sense when we're being unrealistic and react to it. And if they're there to innovate, then being compliant may well feel like the antithesis of what they've been hired to do.

Counter-intuitively – and just between us – having a few breaches on the record might actually be helpful. If no one ever breaks our rules, how do we know we've calibrated them correctly? Perhaps we've allowed our population too much latitude. We shouldn't encourage it, but having people occasionally bend or break our rules can help make sure we've got them right. As we'll see later in the book, there are ways we can use that to our advantage. Of course, that doesn't mean we should tolerate all errors or breaches. As we'll see, there are rules, and there are rules!

Recoverable vs Irrecoverable

So how can we balance the realism of recognising there will be breaches and errors and a need to prevent the worst possible outcomes? For that, we need to turn to Netflix. Not to stream a video but to the company itself.

In 2009, Netflix published a 129-page set of slides entitled "Freedom & Responsibility Culture"[1] in place of a staff handbook. The slides – which must rank among the most downloaded PowerPoint slides ever – were created by Netflix founder Reed Hastings and then Chief Talent Officer Patty McCord. Both have subsequently written books about it, which I highly recommend.

In among slides that explain things like Netflix's hiring and remuneration policy, there are some which outline their approach to compliance. The "c word" doesn't feature, but that's the substance of it. It's a little radical, so it won't be for everyone, but in the spirit of challenging ourselves, I think it's thought-provoking.

Their philosophy is to separate errors into "recoverable" and "irrecoverable" errors. The former are things they'd rather not have happen but from which – as the name suggests – the firm can recover. The latter are things from which it is hard to recover: either "irrecoverable disasters", for example, financial statements containing errors or where hackers steal customer credit card information. Or they are "matters of moral, ethical, or legal principle", for example, preventing dishonesty or harassment.

Implicitly, this means having zero tolerance for irrecoverable things and a relatively high tolerance for recoverable things. This approach leads them to distinguish between a "good" process, which "helps talented people get more done", and a "bad" process, which "tries to prevent recoverable mistakes". As a result – and here's where it gets really interesting – this means the only types of rules you need are those which prevent irrecoverable errors.

I think this is a fascinating approach. Not only is it realistic in recognising things will go wrong, but also that not all rules are equally important. I'm not suggesting that Netflix's model is perfect. In many environments, it won't work. But there are some things we can learn from it.

In Aggregate, Not in Isolation

This brings me back to the rule. When I say that 100% compliance is impossible, I mean in aggregate. I'm not suggesting that we tolerate all mistakes. But we need to accept some. It is perfectly possible to achieve 100% compliance with a particular rule if we throw enough at it. If that weren't the case, we'd regularly be seeing instances of nuclear power stations blowing up. But in a world of finite resources, we can't do that for every rule. Our employees know that as well as we do.

This is why I like the idea behind the Netflix approach. Being open about the distinction between breaches of rules that are recoverable and those that are irrecoverable helps us to manage resources and staff attention. Because for those areas where 100% compliance is not just desirable but necessary, we will need their help to deliver it.

Back to Zero Accidents

This brings me back to the HKSC and their Zero Accidents Policy. I have a sneaking suspicion the HKSC knows it won't get zero accidents. But it sends a powerful signal to stakeholders, particularly their staff, of their primary objective. Zero accidents isn't an irrecoverable error for HKSC, but the philosophy is the same; they're making clear what really matters and focusing on that.

Note

1. https://humanizingrules.link/netflix.

CHAPTER 20
RULE NUMBER THREE

What's the Point of Airport Security?

Next time you're catching a plane, take a closer look at airport security. Not too close, mind you, I don't want you to be detained! On the face of it, the reason we all go through the process is to protect passengers, staff, aircraft, and airports. Yet, as readers who are frequent flyers can attest, there are huge inconsistencies between airports – and indeed individual screenings – in who and what the process rejects or lets through. Fly often enough, and you'll experience false positives; times when you or your bags have required re-scanning for no apparent reason. Equally, you can have times when your bag sails through the scanner, only for you later to discover that it contained an item you'd forgotten was there but which was not within the rules.

There's a lot we could criticise about this. Viewed through a cost-efficiency lens, the security processes can often seem disproportionate, ineffective, or both. Yet, from a psychological perspective, there's a good argument to be made for designing them that way. What look like random and inefficient processes can – though this is not always the case – serve a useful purpose that might not be immediately obvious.

Those apparent inefficiencies aren't accidental. They're designed in a way that not only does the apparent job of screening passengers but also sends subliminal signals to two very different audiences:

The first audience is "bad actors" – people intentionally setting out to cause harm – for whom the signal is a deterrent. Not only does the existence of the check increase the risk of getting caught, but the random and inefficient nature of the controls creates additional uncertainty. If you're trying to circumvent a process, not being entirely sure how that process might play out makes life somewhat harder.

The second audience is the average passenger, for whom the security check is intended to provide reassurance that it is safe to travel. The inconvenience of the process makes it far more memorable and salient – a word that we discussed in Chapter 15, which in this context means "noticeable" – than it would be if the process were slicker.

In both cases, the process isn't just there to serve its ostensible purpose. It's also there to serve a psychological one. Not convinced? Try this thought exercise: imagine you had a choice between flying with an airline with no security checks and one with standard security checks. Assuming they charged a similar price for a similar experience, which one would you go for? Most of us, I suspect, would opt for the one with security, even if we thought the process wasn't perfect.

Welcome to the Theatre

Exercises like airport security, which contain a performative element, are sometimes referred to as "Theatre", as in security theatre, safety theatre, or compliance theatre. They're the reason we have Rule Number Three:

If you're putting on a show, know your audience(s).

On the one hand, this sounds very obvious. Yet, as we'll see, Theatre comes in many forms. Whether you know it or not, you're probably deploying Theatre in your organisation. That's one of the challenges with Theatre; because we don't always recognise that we're putting it on, we don't think to review whether it is delivering the desired objective. Equally, we may miss other opportunities to put on a show.

In this rule, I'm going to highlight some examples of Theatre to help you think about where you're using it, either knowingly or unknowingly. Once you know what Theatre is and some of the ways in which it works, you can use the ideas in this book to help you think about how your audiences are likely to react.

Note that the word audience(s) in the Rule can be plural. Often there will only be one audience. But more often than not – as we saw with the airport – there will be more than one. Sometimes, we'll want to communicate with all of them. On other occasions, we may just be targeting one of them, in which case, we need to consider its impact on other audiences – whether intended or unintended – and whether that matters.

ROK Ready Theatre

On a visit to Seoul a few years ago, I visited the Demilitarised Zone (DMZ) between North and South Korea. It's a fascinating place, full of historical significance. You can feel the tension in the air. The South Korean military police officers who stand guard in the DMZ are specially selected for their imposing physical presence and martial arts skills.

To maximise their physical stature, the officers are trained to adopt a position known as "ROK Ready" (short for Republic of Korea), a modified taekwondo pose. They also put ball bearings in their trouser turn-ups, making a very loud noise while walking. It's pure Theatre, explicitly designed to intimidate the North Koreans.

It's very effective. I know this because even though I wasn't the intended audience for the ROK Ready Theatre, it really had an impact on me; I was utterly terrified! Even though the officers were, in part, there to protect visitors like me! It did mean that I did exactly as I was told, an unintended but desirable consequence.

Deterrent Theatre

Regulators and police forces frequently use Theatre to try to stop people from breaking the law. A prominent example of this kind of deterrent is the "perp walk" where someone who has been arrested is deliberately walked through a prominent location to send a warning to other potential rulebreakers.

They also pursue high-profile cases just to make a point. In October 2022, social media influencer Kim Kardashian was fined $1.26m by the SEC for advertising a cryptocurrency without disclosing that she had been paid to do so. In bringing the case, the SEC had two audiences in mind. The first were influencers who might seek to do similar promotions. Seeing Kardashian being fined would hopefully deter them. The second was the general public, who might invest in schemes promoted by celebrities.

What's clever about this Theatre is that it deployed Kardashian's profile and notoriety to regulatory advantage, buying them the kind of publicity that would not usually be available on the SEC's marketing budget. While she didn't directly "endorse" the SEC's message, the effect was similar. Far more people have heard about the regulation and the risks of cryptocurrencies than would have been the case if they hadn't fined such a high-profile person. At the same time, the SEC showed social media savvy of their own by releasing an engaging YouTube video warning of the risks of celebrity endorsements of financial products.

Role Model Theatre

Theatre can also be used to encourage people to do things. Role modelling of desirable behaviours is an excellent example of this. In 1911, London Underground used an "influencer" to persuade passengers to use escalators, which they'd just introduced. At the time, escalators were a relatively new idea, so people were nervous about using them, particularly on the Underground, where the stairs were long and steep.

To persuade passengers that they were safe to use, the transport authorities followed an important advertising principle: "don't tell people, show them". They hired William "Bumper" Harris, a one-legged man, to ride up and down the escalators. The idea was that if a one-legged man felt safe enough doing it, so should everyone else. Bumper was paid to ride up and down the escalators for a few days to demonstrate how safe they were. It did the trick! Once people got used to using them, social proof took over. You can, incidentally, see a tiny statue of Bumper on a model escalator in London's Transport Museum.

Role Model Theatre is also very susceptible to backfiring if those putting it on don't stick to the script. We've all attended training programmes introduced by a senior person who is there to say something like, "This training is incredibly important." So you'll know how they behave afterwards is even more important. Because then you get to see how important it actually is to them. If they tell the staff it is important and then immediately leave or stay but play on their phone the whole time, that signals that it really isn't that important.

My favourite ever example was someone senior who turned up to say how critical the training was but then couldn't remember the subject. They finished their little speech by saying, "So, enjoy this training, I'm off to do something really important, so I can't stick around!"

Box-Ticking Theatre

There's a joke in the UK that the monarch must think the world smells of fresh paint. That's because whenever they go somewhere on a visit, a clean-up operation happens beforehand, which usually includes a new coat of paint. Depending on your perspective, this is either great because it gives people a reason to do the clean-up; or a waste of time and money because it's only being done for show. I can see both arguments.

Replace the word "monarch" with regulator, auditor, or inspector, and you've got an even more commonly observed form of Theatre. The idea behind this type of show is obvious: convince the audience that things are under control. On the face of it, it makes perfect sense. But it's worth remembering that any employees asked to help put on the Theatre are also being sent a signal: that it's OK to "window dress". That could lead to them doing the same thing internally. If you're teaching people how to act, they may put on a show for you!

Backstage Tour

One of the ways we can put on Theatre is to take a process that might usually be hidden and make it visible; what you might think of as a backstage tour. Visit a restaurant toilet, and you're likely to see a log on the wall which records when it was last cleaned. The primary purpose of the schedule is to allow the manager to check that the toilets have been cleaned regularly.

But it's also there to serve as a piece of Theatre designed to signal to customers that the establishment takes hygiene seriously. That matters in the context of a restaurant because customers want to know their meal is being prepared in a clean environment by people who take food hygiene seriously. As a result, highlighting to customers how clean the toilets are, serves as a proxy for how clean the kitchen is. If the toilets – which they can see – are dirty, then the kitchen – which they can't – might also be dirty.

There's usually also a clue that this is their intention. When we see words on the log along the following lines – "Please let our staff know if the toilets need cleaning" – we know we're supposed to see it. Cynics might respond to the request for customers to report unclean toilets with, "If you were keeping a proper eye on it, you'd know and wouldn't need to ask for my help!"

Of course, the Theatre is only compelling from a customer perspective if the toilets *are* actually clean. If they're not, we've been given a clear signal that hygiene is not a top priority. In this case, we might leave or choose to experiment by reporting it and seeing how they react.

The Toilet Theatre also has a second audience: the staff. Putting the log where customers can see it also reminds them that a failure to clean the toilet regularly or adequately will be visible to customers.

When the Scenery Falls

Sometimes, backstage tours are given unintentionally. If you've ever asked to leave your luggage in a hotel and been shown to a room behind reception where you can leave it, chances are you've had a glimpse backstage. When that happens, you're likely to see things intended for staff eyes only.

My top tip is always to read the staff notices. Because they're not designed to be read by guests, they're unfiltered. You'll learn far more about how much the hotel really cares about customer service, cleanliness, and safety than you will from reading what they want you to.

Of course, that does highlight the possibility of the mischievous option of "accidentally on purpose" leaving backstage insights visible to the audience. If you've seen the movie *Operation Mincemeat*, which is the true story of a British deception operation in the Second World War, that served to disguise the 1943 Allied Invasion of Sicily, you'll have some idea how that might work. Since we're not at war with our employees, I recommend avoiding such tactics.

Finally, be aware that Theatre is often used as an excuse for poorly designed, inefficient processes. I've lost count of the number of times when I've been told that things can't be changed because "that's what the regulator expects to see", even when the process makes no sense whatsoever. That's not Theatre that anyone should be putting on.

CHAPTER 21
RULE NUMBER FOUR

Have You Ever...?

If there's one thing guaranteed to make me smile during a long flight, it's those entry forms you must complete to be allowed into your destination country. You know, the ones that ask long lists of yes/no questions and provide boxes that are either disproportionately over- or undersized for the answers you're being asked to give. Enjoy them while you still can because many countries are replacing them with online pre-approval processes, and in doing so, they're removing many of the most entertaining questions.

Sadly, my personal favourite from all my years of travelling, US Visa Waiver Form I-94W, has already been retired. The more recent version was also a bit too sensible for my liking. It's the classic edition from the early 2000s that I really enjoyed. Readers who travelled to the US at that time may remember it as the green form that asked some wonderfully odd questions, like:

> B. ... are you seeking entry to engage in criminal or immoral activities?

> C. Have you ever been or are you now involved in espionage or sabotage; or in terrorist activities; or genocide; or between 1933 and 1945 were involved, in any way, in persecutions associated with Nazi Germany or its allies?

Has anyone, I used to wonder to myself, ever answered "yes" to either question? If so, it's very likely they either did so by mistake or because they're auditioning to be the subject of the next Dunning and Kruger research project (see Chapter 6). Though, come to think of it, you can see why they might want to keep those people out of the country!

You'd be incredibly unlikely to find someone who, if they were being honest about their intentions, would answer "yes". Apart, of course, from Mr Logic. But would anyone ever think, "You know what, I am seeking entry to engage in criminal and immoral activities. I wasn't going to tell you, but now that you've asked me that question, I can't possibly lie on the form"?

Immigration Logic

What *was* the point of those questions? Presumably, there was one. I'm a firm believer in a principle called Chesterton's Fence, which suggests that one should never make changes to processes or rules until one understands why they were put there in the first place. Since I don't understand the logic, I'm reluctant to be overly critical. However, I've had a lot of time to think about this while flying to the US, and decades later, it's still unclear what it might be. I can see that the questions could strengthen the legal case against someone who subsequently turned out to have been travelling to the US for those banned purposes, but... I could go on, but you get the idea.

The reason I'm reminiscing about my failure to understand Form I-94W isn't that I've suddenly worked it out. Instead, it's so that I can highlight how the thinking behind it – the immigration logic that I still find so baffling – is frequently used in other contexts, including compliance.

As we've seen, sometimes, when you change contexts, things that didn't make sense suddenly do. Applying what I call "Form I-94W Logic" to compliance isn't one of those. I'll explain what I mean by highlighting some of the implicit presumptions that result from using "immigration logic" and why they're not necessarily a good thing.

How "Bad" People React

The first implicit presumption of Form I-94W Logic is that "bad" people can be swayed by "due process", which means the rules and norms that the rest of us follow. Hence they'll do what I suggested they wouldn't and feel compelled by the persuasive powers of Form I-94W to tell the truth about their evil intentions.

While we might smile at someone intending to engage in criminal or immoral activities ticking the "yes" box on the immigration form, many compliance processes use precisely that logic. Not only – as we will see – are these processes designed around a flawed presumption about the risk we're seeking to mitigate, but they're also often not very effective.

Someone deliberately setting out to break the rules isn't going to listen to what we tell them on a training course. The whole idea of training only works if, on some level, the person being trained wants to learn. Intentional rulebreakers are also not going to read policies; unless, as we'll see, they're doing it to find loopholes or "air cover" for noncompliance (see Chapter 22). I'm reminded of that quote from the judge in the Adoboli trial: "the real characteristic of the rogue trader is that he ignores the rules designed to manage risk" (see the Introduction).

People intent on doing "bad" things are likely to think they are "above the law". Like former UK Prime Minister Boris Johnson, who, while in office, showed a disregard for standard conventions and resigned after a series of ethical scandals. Tellingly, a 17-year-old Johnson was described in his school report, by his then Headmaster Martin Hammond, in the following terms:

Boris really has adopted a disgracefully cavalier attitude to his classical studies. [He] sometimes seems affronted when criticised for what amounts to a gross failure of responsibility (and surprised at the same time that he was not appointed Captain of the school for the next half). I think he honestly believes that it is churlish of us not to regard him as an exception, one who should be free of the network of obligation that binds everyone else.

If we want to prevent the "bad" people, we will need different tools than the ones we use for "good" people. Literally and metaphorically, they're not playing by the same rules as the rest of us. Arguably, they're not even playing the same game.

That doesn't mean that everything we currently do is ineffective. Some techniques we deploy that work on "good" people will also help deter "bad" people. But others won't, and some might even be counter-productive. To quote the famous line from the movie *Jaws*, "You're gonna need a bigger boat". Otherwise, we risk approaching it like the question on Form I-94W that no one will answer in the affirmative. It seems sensible in theory but risks failing in practice.

"Bad" People vs "Good" People

The second implicit presumption of Form I-94W Logic is that to achieve compliance, we need to eliminate human risk by stopping the "bad" people from doing "bad" things. To be fair to Form I-94W, it doesn't go that far, but it's pointing in that general direction! On one level, this is, of course, true. Whenever things go wrong in organisations, a human component is involved; either causing the problem or making it worse. Whenever things go badly wrong – the types of incidents where the CEO resigns or gets fired – the narrative *is* usually about an individual or group of individuals who are responsible.

But not all "bad" things are caused by "bad" people. Though perhaps it's not surprising we tend to think this way. After all, it's the essence of children's fairytales which present us with a polarised world where Harry Potter (good) fights Voldemort (bad), or Cinderella (good) outwits the Wicked Stepmother (there's even a clue in her name: bad). In the real world, it's not that simple. We also need to target the "good" people who do "bad" things.

In Chapter 4, I introduced Professor Yuval Feldman, the author of *The Law of Good People*,[1] which explores why, rather than writing laws for bad people, we should write them for good people. As I was beginning my journey of bringing behavioural science to ethics and compliance, it was a book that hugely inspired me; it continues to do so today. In an interview talking about the book, Professor Feldman explains:

We have a misconstrued perception of who the "bad guys" are. In reality, (almost) all of us are violators of laws, regulations, contracts and ethical norms. Various studies on the causes of such "ordinary unethically", including insurance fraud, employee theft, and tax evasion, suggest how prevalent, mindless, and sometimes banal wrongdoing can be.

We're misdiagnosing the problem by considering compliance as needed to stop "bad" people from doing "bad" things. There are "bad" people who deliberately set out to do the wrong thing, but they are a tiny minority. As are the people who will always do the right thing, who won't cause you an obvious compliance problem, but are an outlier worth keeping an eye on from time to time.

The vast majority of people sit between those two extremes; they'll generally try to do the right thing, but they're also capable of being influenced in the opposite direction. That means we need to think about them and treat them not as "bad" people to be prevented from doing "bad" things, but as "good" people who need our help to do the right things. Which is what Professor Feldman's book title is driving towards; rather than writing laws – or in our case, rules — for "bad" people, we need to write them for "good" people. Or, as I like to think of it:

Design for the willing, not for the wilful.

How "Good" People React

The third implicit presumption is that processes that deter "bad" people from doing "bad" things won't have side effects. If that reminds you of the Theatre I explored in the last Rule; then you're on the right lines.

Before I explore that, be aware that the phrase "side effect" I used two sentences ago is highly misleading. There is no such thing as a "side effect"; every outcome of a behavioural intervention is an effect. Framing the ones we find undesirable as "side effects" might help us to downplay them, but they're as much a part of the intervention as the desired effects.

Back to the Theatre! As a "good" person, I read my favourite version of Form I-94W and laugh at what I perceive to be the ridiculousness of the questions. Since I'm naturally curious, I wonder what on earth the purpose is and conclude that the process makes no sense. That doesn't make me think more positively about the people who have designed the form.

In an immigration context, it doesn't matter what I think. Since I'm not ticking those boxes, they're not designed for me. Whether they're genuine questions or, in the terminology of Rule Number Three, "Legal Theatre", I'm not the intended audience. If I want to travel to the US, I'm forced to follow the US Customs & Border Protection (CBP) protocols. Regardless of what I think of those protocols, it's their country, so I must follow their rules.[2]

But in a compliance context, a very different dynamic is at play; because there's a need for a good relationship between the rule setter and the rule taker. Unlike my interactions with CBP, which are transactional, compliance requires a more relationship-based approach. As we've seen, many things we need our employees to do rely on their goodwill; or, at the very least, their acceptance.

If we design compliance processes for "bad" people, we'll do things that we wouldn't do if we were designing them for "good" people. For example, a process for "bad" people might intentionally send a signal that they're not trusted. But if we also send that same signal to "good" people, we risk them responding in kind.

Declassify Form I-94W

This brings me back to the Rule. If we want to succeed in meeting our objectives, then we need to design our processes for those who, on some level, want to comply with them. We then need separate processes to deter and catch those who don't. In the spirit of Professor Feldman's book, we should write rules for "good" people and design governance processes to deal with "bad" ones.

In the meantime, I'm looking forward to the day they declassify the papers about Form I-94W, so I can find out what secrets those questions are hiding!

Notes

1. Yuval Feldman, *The Law of Good People* (Cambridge: Cambridge University Press, 2018).

2. It's one of the reasons we need to be careful about Compliance acting as the enforcer of rules. If you're the person who can hand out punishment, then you're probably not the person I'm going to want to speak to, to get strategic advice. I don't get strategic advice from a parking warden.

CHAPTER 22
RULE NUMBER FIVE

Ever Stuck

In March 2021, a 200,000-ton container ship called the *Ever Given* made news headlines around the world when it got stuck in the Suez Canal. A journey that should have taken around 13 hours, ended up taking over six days, during which time the *Ever Given* blocked the main shipping route from the Atlantic to the Indian Ocean. In doing so, it caused a tailback of over 200 vessels and disrupted global supply chains. You might not remember the name of the ship, but you'll probably remember seeing pictures of an enormous cargo boat run aground on a sand bank being dug out by what looked like a toy digger.

Like me, your initial reaction upon hearing the story or seeing the image of it stuck, was probably to blame the captain for what seems like a basic navigation error. To misquote Brian Cullinan's famous words, "It doesn't sound very complicated, but you have to make sure you're steering the ship straight down the canal" (see the Introduction). But then I discovered that ships travelling through the Suez Canal are required by law to have a local pilot on board to help guide them through it. All of a sudden, I drew an entirely different conclusion. Surely, I now reasoned, it must be the pilot's fault. After all, preventing that kind of incident is the sole reason they're there.

Until that is, I learned that this wasn't the first time the *Ever Given* had been involved in an accident. Just over a year before the *Ever Given* got stuck in the Suez Canal, it was leaving the German port of Hamburg, when it moved too close to a pontoon and hit a local passenger ferry. Fortunately no one was killed or injured. Reading about this and looking at the pictures of it, I began to see the Suez incident as part of a pattern, rather than a one-off freak accident.

Then, as I was writing this book in early 2022, news broke that the *Ever Forward* – like the *Ever Given*, a ship owned by the Evergreen Marine Corporation – had strayed outside normal shipping lanes and run aground in shallow water off Chesapeake Bay in Maryland. It took an entire month before the *Ever Forward* could once again live up to its name.

Why, I began to wonder, was a company operating ships that seemed to be so difficult to steer? Then it occurred to me that someone had to design and build the ships in the first place; what on earth were they thinking? Perhaps, I reasoned, it wasn't the fault of the pilots or the captains after all, but rather with the design of the ships. So I did some more investigating. It turns out that these aren't the only recent accidents involving cargo ships owned by that company. In 2017, for example, the *Ever Smart* lost a large number of containers mid-ocean.

But then the Evergreen Marine Corporation is by no means the only shipping company to suffer incidents of this kind. It's far more common than we might think. It's just that the *Ever Given* provided a "made for news" visual spectacle, that means any incident involving an Evergreen Marine ship has now automatically become newsworthy.

The Bigger Picture

One the one hand, my (pun intended) voyage of discovery about the *Ever Given* is a perfect illustration of WYSIATI in action (see Chapter 8). But it also illustrates the power of looking at a series of data points, rather than individual ones.

Every time I discovered new information about the story, my perspective on who was to blame for the incident changed. Of course, I'm no maritime expert, so it is perfectly possible, I'm joining dots that I shouldn't. But even if the insights I discovered, aren't as relevant as I've suggested, knowing that the incidents in Chesapeake Bay and Hamburg happened must, on some level, also be useful when we're analysing the Suez incident.

Just as I had initially held the captain responsible for the Suez incident, our inclination, when we hear that someone has broken a rule, is often to blame them. This makes perfect sense. After all, it is their actions, or inactions, that have caused the rule to be broken. And it is important to hold people to account for their decisions.

Obviously, we need to investigate individual incidents as and when they occur, particularly when they're on the scale of the Suez one. But if we want to build a more robust compliance framework, it's important to also look at where similar events are occurring to see what lessons we can learn.

The Power of the Collective

In that spirit, Rule Number Five encourages us to look at collective, rather than individual, behaviours. In other words, to look at situations where lots of people aren't doing what we want them to. It reads as follows:

> If one person breaks a rule you've got a people problem. If lots of people break a rule, you've got a rule problem.

The basis for the rule is that if the majority of people are able to comply with a rule and one person isn't, then that suggests there's an issue with the individual. But if lots of people aren't complying with a rule, then it's unlikely that they've all set out to deliberately break it.

After all, you're unlikely to have lots of people deliberately setting out to break a rule. There must be some explanation as to why it's happening. That needn't mean the rule itself is a problem; though it might be. Perhaps the reason for the noncompliance is that the rule looks good in theory, but is incredibly hard to comply with in practice. It might be that the training on the rule is inadequate, or the systems people need to use to comply with it are confusing. Whatever the reason, the fact that lots of people aren't complying is a clue that something needs to be looked at.

The other reason for that is that if the "rule" – by which I mean the rule itself, or the training, or communications about the rule, etc. – has a problem that isn't fixed, then you're just asking for the same problem to reappear. As Alexander den Heijer, a Dutch psychologist puts it: "When a flower doesn't bloom, you fix the environment in which it grows, not the flower." The risk in not fixing the problem, and concluding it must all be the fault of the individuals concerned, is that you could get rid of all the people, hire new ones, and the same problem could occur again.

The Wisdom of the Crowd

Another benefit in focussing on collective behaviours is that we can deploy resources more appropriately. If one person is breaking a rule, and everyone else isn't, then we can respond accordingly. But if the problem is more widespread, it is worth deploying resources to do a detailed investigation, because we can see there is something in or around the rule that must, on some level, be contributing to the compliance problem. In other words – whisper it! – it's not entirely the fault of those who aren't complying.

To look at this another way, we're using the same logic we use when we consult Tripadvisor, and channelling the "wisdom" of the crowd. Of course, when lots of people break a rule, it doesn't feel as if they are displaying wisdom, but on some level there will be a reason for what they are doing. If we can work that out, we can stop or deter others from doing the same thing. Because we're using collective breaches to inform us, we've got more data and we're more likely to be able to identify the reasons why they are occurring. In simple terms, that also means we've got more people we can talk to about what's happening.

Ergodicity

On of the reasons we want to look at collective behaviour is that averages can be misleading. To help illustrate this, let me introduce a concept called ergodicity.

Imagine we ask 100 people to each roll a dice once and record their result. Then, we ask one person to roll a dice 100 times and record the results. In both cases, we'd expect to get the same outcome. There's no reason why 100 people rolling one dice each should produce a different result to one person rolling a dice 100 times.

Now imagine, we play a game of Russian roulette. For those unfamiliar with it, it's a "game" that involves loading a single round in a revolver. The person playing then spins the cylinder and points the revolver at their head and pulls the trigger. There's a one in six chance of being killed or seriously injured. While we might be able to persuade someone to play the game once, we're unlikely to be able to persuade them to play it lots of times. Unlike the dice game, there's a huge difference in outcomes between one person playing Russian roulette six times, and six people playing Russian roulette once.

In an ergodic world, the expected value of an activity performed by a group is the same as that for an individual carrying out that activity on their own. The dice roll game is ergodic; Russian roulette is non-ergodic.

Removing "Air Cover"

Eliminating the impediments to compliance that we learn from looking at collective behaviour has one further benefit: it removes what I call "air cover" from people who are wilfully or negligently noncompliant. If there are lots of people who are not complying with a particular rule, for reasons we could prevent, then they are acting as air cover for those who are doing it for different reasons.

Imagine lots of people aren't complying with a rule and we discover that it is likely to be down to a system that is hard to use. If we don't fix that system, then we provide air cover to those who are failing to comply because they can't be bothered. Not just in terms of giving them an excuse, but also when we review compliance risks, they will be "lumped in" with the others. Solving the problem will ensure we isolate their behaviour. To put it another way, if we make it easier for people to be compliant, then we'll know that those who aren't are more likely to be doing it wilfully, and we can react accordingly.

It's the Stupid, System

Now I'm going to share a case study that illustrates how this Rule works in practice. A Financial Services client of mine had a compliance problem with a rule which required employees who wanted to trade listed shares to obtain permission before doing so. These are standard within the industry and the concept behind them is widely understood.

Since people in the industry can, in the course of their work, be in possession of price-sensitive non-public information, the firm can prevent staff from trading if there's a risk of an actual or perceived conflict of interest. It's not a rule that people would be unfamiliar with, or that is in any way complex. Yet large numbers of their employees were simply failing to comply with it.

The solution the client had proposed was entirely logical. Any employees who had breached the policy would be disciplined, and required to do further training on the relevant rules. A firm-wide email would also be sent, reminding everyone of the policy.

In the spirit of this rule, I suggested that we look in a little more detail to see whether there were any obvious patterns to the breaches. It turned out that in the majority of cases, it was the identical story. The shares those employees had been trading were the company's own. For entirely legitimate reasons, staff were selling shares awarded to them as deferred bonuses, on or just after on the day the shares vested; in other words, at the earliest possible moment.

Under the firm's rules, this required pre-approval. Yet the system they needed to use to sell the shares – which was built internally – didn't warn anyone trying to sell shares that they would need permission. Nor was there any control to ensure they actually had permission. Suddenly, it was possible to see why some people might reasonably have concluded that because the system allowed it, they didn't need separate pre-approval.

In theory, the staff should have known they needed pre-approval to trade. But, in practice, it is easy to see how they might not have thought about it. Not least, because the timing of the share sale wasn't their choice; they didn't want shares they'd been forced to hold, they wanted cash, so were keen to sell as soon as possible. The fact that lots of people broke the rule suggested it was more confusion than malicious intent driving the action. It's also worth remembering that if someone were going to be engaging in insider dealing, they'd be unlikely to do it on a system owned by their employer; they'd go "off the grid".

All of which led me to suggest that they focus on changing the system. By all means, discipline people who should have known the rules, but why not prevent others making the same mistake? So, that's what they did. A warning was added to the system and, as a result, numbers of breaches of that rule declined substantially. There was a further benefit: management time was no longer wasted by looking at alarming statistics; and if breaches of that policy did occur, they knew they'd removed one obvious excuse.

CHAPTER 23
RULE NUMBER SIX

Jurassic Park but for Komodo Dragons

In December 2020, a 46-year-old man called Elias Agas was rushed to hospital after being seriously injured at a construction site on Rinca Island in Indonesia. Rinca is part of Komodo National Park, a UNESCO World Heritage Site home to the world's only population of Komodo dragons. The Indonesian government referred to the project Agas was working on as a "premium tourism spot"; or to put it another way, a place that tourists will be able to visit to see Komodo dragons.

In case you're unfamiliar with them, Komodo dragons are wild lizards that can grow up to 3 metres in length. They have razor-sharp teeth that allow them to administer a venomous bite that lowers blood pressure, causes massive bleeding, prevents blood clotting, and induces shock. In other words, a very dangerous animal indeed, as Agas discovered.

The project – which I'll refer to as Komodo Park – has been dubbed "Jurassic Park for Komodo dragons", after the famous book and movie by Michael Crichton. On the face of it, that sounds unfair. After all, *Jurassic Park* is a fictional account of a private business that brings dinosaurs back to life, where things go disastrously wrong. Komodo Park is a government initiative to build a visitor centre for an endangered species.

Until I tell you that a promotional video for Komodo Park uses imagery that closely resembles the movie version of *Jurassic Park* and the actual theme music from the movie.[1] In other words, a fictional story designed to warn of the risks of turning dangerous animals into theme park attractions is being used as an inspiration for the real thing. The only difference is that they're not resurrecting an extinct species; they're using an endangered one.

Those responsible for the development of Komodo Park – which was still under construction at the time of writing – would do well to familiarise themselves with one of *Jurassic Park*'s most famous quotes. It's where scientist Doctor Ian Malcolm, an expert in Chaos Theory, played by Jeff Goldblum, who has been invited to the park to give his blessing, says, "Your scientists were so preoccupied with whether or not they could, they didn't stop to think if they should."

That quote and the thinking behind Komodo Park provide the perfect illustration of Rule Number Seven:

Just because you can, doesn't mean you should.

While the Rule is very simple, it is also crucial because, as we saw in Chapter 5, our Judge brain is capable of coming up with excuses for decisions the Gator brain has already taken. If we don't, in the words of Ian Malcolm in *Jurassic Park*, stop to consider whether we should do something, it's likely we'll already have reached for a ready-made excuse that we could do it.

It is also worth noting that the Rule has broad application since it is not just relevant to our decision-making as we seek to impose rules on our employees; it applies equally to theirs when they decide how or whether to comply with them.

On the one hand, we need to think carefully about whether and, if so, how we should impose rules on our employees. Just because we have legal rights doesn't mean it's right for us to do so. On the other hand, they need to think about how they interpret rules. Sometimes, the rules permit them to do things they know aren't right.

Compliance Meets Ethics

The rule points to natural tension between compliance and ethics in both cases. I'm often asked why many organisations have functions that combine both disciplines. After all, there's a clear distinction between the intrinsic nature of "ethics" – principles that we uphold because we believe them to be right – and the extrinsic nature of "compliance", rules imposed on the firm from outside. My answer is that the two are interrelated because many regulations are designed to deliver ethical outcomes.

It's also essential for employees not to distinguish between "things we do because we're told to" and "things we do because we think they're important". Otherwise, we risk giving them the impression that we don't think regulations are essential. That matters because of the way we can all – myself included – find ourselves justifying our decision-making when we're either breaking a rule or doing something unethical.

The two main justifications we often turn to are as follows:

1. If we want to justify doing something that breaks a rule, we tend to do so by referencing ethics.

2. Conversely, if we want to justify something unethical, we tend to do so by reference to compliance.

Before I explain what I mean by this, please note the word "tend" in both justifications. I'm not saying this happens all the time. I'm just saying it happens a lot. With that in mind, here's a simple example of how we might use ethics to justify noncompliance. If the speed limit is 70 and we want to drive at 90 – in other words, we're trying to justify a compliance breach – then we might seek to explain it by referencing the fact it was the middle of the night and there was no other traffic. In simple terms, the "spirit of the law" wasn't being broken because we weren't putting any other road users in danger.

Or, we might try to explain it by reference to why we needed to get to our destination; perhaps we were racing to the airport to catch a plane, or we had an urgent medical appointment. Both are "the ends justify the means" excuses that seek to explain why the rules shouldn't apply in this specific situation. Alternatively, from "the dog ate my homework" school of excuses, we might opt for something like "the speed limit wasn't obvious on that stretch of road, so I didn't realise I was speeding". It's a clear attempt to paint breaking the limit as ethical because we didn't know we were doing it. Implicitly, if we had known, we wouldn't have been speeding!

Then, there's the opposite: using compliance to justify unethical behaviour. If the speed limit is 70, but we know that the weather conditions mean it is dangerous to drive more than 50, then we might justify driving 60 by reference to the limit.

From an ethical perspective, we understand that we shouldn't be driving at that speed, but we also know that the rules clearly permit us to do so. This is also known as a "where does it say that I can't do that?" type of excuse when people point to the law when confronted by their own unethical behaviour.

COM-B: how Capability, Opportunity, Motivation drives Behaviour

To help us to think about this further, I'm going to take this opportunity to introduce you to a simple behavioural model that I often use with clients. The model is called COM-B and is designed to be a simple overview of what drives behaviour. Although it is intended for use in driving behavioural change, we can also use it to analyse why people are engaging in particular behaviours. In other words, it's a design tool and a diagnostic tool.

Professor Susan Michie and her colleagues at University College, London developed COM-B.[2] If you are interested in this area, I recommend looking at their Behavioural Change Wheel, a more complex framework that builds on COM-B.

The idea behind COM-B is that there are three main components to any Behaviour (B). For a behaviour to occur, an individual needs to feel:

- they are psychologically and physically able to do so – in other words, they have the Capability (C);

- they have the social and physical opportunity to engage in the behaviour – Opportunity (O);

- they want or need to carry out the behaviour – Motivation (M).

The elements are interdependent; Capability and Opportunity feed into Motivation, which drives Behaviour. For example, if we want to run the Tokyo marathon, we need to be physically and mentally prepared (C), have an allocated place (O), and be motivated to run the race (M). On the day, we also obviously need to be in Tokyo at the start at our allotted time (O).

We may find that being allocated a place makes us more likely to feel motivated, even if we know that we are not yet physically or mentally prepared. Equally, even without the allocated place, the fact we are physically and mentally ready can motivate us. However, turning up for the start of the race without an entry – in other words, a critical element of O is missing – cannot be compensated for by the fact we would be able to physically run the race.

Applying COM-B to the Rule lets us see that "can" in "because you can" is a function of both Capability and Opportunity, whereas "should" in "you should" is a function of Motivation.

I'll end this rule with another story. It's incredibly well known – which, as you'll see, is deeply ironic given the story's subject – but even if you know it, I think it helps to underpin another aspect of this rule.

The Streisand Effect

Readers of a certain age will be familiar with the multimillion record-selling singer Barbra Streisand. Younger readers, who may not know her music, are more likely to have heard of her thanks to something called the Streisand Effect. It's the name given to a behavioural dynamic she helped to make famous.

In 2003, Streisand sued a photographer called Kenneth Adelman for $50 million for violation of privacy. Adelman took a series of photographs of the Pacific coastline from a helicopter for the California Coastal Records Project to document coastal erosion. Streisand, whose Malibu beach house was visible in one of the photos, went to court to get it taken down. Not only did she lose her case, but in taking legal action, she inadvertently drew attention to the very thing she was trying to hide.

Before the lawsuit, the image showing a somewhat blurry photo of Streisand's house had been downloaded just six times. Two of those times were by Streisand's lawyers. Thanks mainly to the publicity generated, it has been viewed millions of times. It's also given us the term the "Streisand Effect". We use it to describe when efforts to keep something secret – usually via the courts – have precisely the opposite effect.

Of course, Streisand was perfectly entitled to sue Adelman. But that didn't mean she was right to do so. In his ruling,[3] the judge noted that "occasional overflights are among those ordinary incidents of community life of which [Barbra Streisand] is a part". He also pointed out that Streisand had previously opened her home to reporters and photographers, so she hadn't always prioritised her own privacy. I would imagine that, with hindsight, Streisand wouldn't have gone ahead with her court case.

That story brings us to the end of the Six Rules. In Part IV, we'll explore RADAR, a BeSci framework that can help you to think about where you might best be able to deploy behavioural interventions.

Notes

1. https://humanizingrules.link/komodo.

2. Susan Michie, Maartje M. van Stralen, and Robert West, "The behaviour change wheel: A new method for characterising and designing behaviour change interventions", *Implementation Science*, 6(1) (2011). doi:10.1186/1748-5908-6-42.

3. https://humanizingrules.link/streisand.

PART IV
RADAR

CHAPTER 24
INTRODUCING RADAR

Where Do I Begin?

So far, we've introduced the basics of behavioural science, explored the Six Rules and learnt about HUMANS, a practical framework. You're now ready to deploy BeSci within your organisation. But where should you begin? There are lots of problems you could theoretically use BeSci to help solve. But if you're going to try something different – perhaps even counter-intuitive or counter-cultural – then you want to maximise your chances of success, particularly if you're subject to a lot of regulatory scrutiny.

In this part of the book, I'm going to suggest some areas where you might like to focus your efforts to increase your chances of success. I'll do that using a framework called RADAR, designed to help you locate "low-hanging fruit" and hopefully get quicker results.

Introducing RADAR

RADAR is based on a very simple idea; since we're trying to influence the decision-making of our employees, why not use them as human "radars" to help guide what we do? We can target our behavioural interventions more effectively by identifying where they are either already noncompliant or showing signs of the potential for noncompliance.

Of course, we can begin with areas where we already have evidence of noncompliance, for example, where we know that there are frequent breaches of a particular rule or policy. But we can also look for behavioural patterns that suggest areas where we have breaches that we might not be aware of, for example, breaches of the "spirit" rather than the "letter" of the law or breaches in areas we're not actively monitoring. We can also use behavioural patterns as forward-looking indicators of where our framework might come under stress.

Movie fans familiar with the science fiction action film, *Minority Report*, starring Tom Cruise, can rest assured that I'm not proposing replicating that dystopian vision of the future. If you've not seen the movie, the plot revolves around PreCrime, a police programme that aims to arrest criminals before they've committed a crime using clairvoyant predictions. While RADAR is predictive, it targets collective rather than individual behaviour patterns, and we're not relying on the vision of three clairvoyants!

Instead, we'll look for what poker players call "tells".[1] These will allow us to identify behavioural dynamics that might indicate potential future areas of noncompliance. For example, a rule we know employees find annoying could be one they choose to circumvent when under pressure.

RADAR consists of five behavioural elements, or "radars", that can help us to look for "tells" that may be worthy of further investigation. Each radar encourages us to look at a different behavioural dynamic.

Collective Not Individual

RADAR is designed for use in determining collective rather than individual behaviour. In doing so, it complies with the spirit of Human Rule Number Five: "if one person breaks a rule, you've got a people problem, but if lots of people break a rule, you've got a rule problem". If we expend effort in reviewing our programme and making changes, we want to do so on things that will work on a broad population, not on individuals who might be outliers.

As I outlined in Rule Number Five, we're not looking to target individual bad actors. We're looking at using the "wisdom of the crowd" to identify where we can change our programme to support most of our employees who generally want to do the right thing. Preventing bad actors is an entirely different challenge.

It's worth being aware that a natural consequence of using behavioural tells as radars is that we will generally identify important things from the employees' perspective, not ours. Some of the framework radars – for example, the first one, which looks at where we have evidence of breaches of our rules – will, by default, highlight things about which we care. However, the later radars, which are predictive, could well highlight things we think are less essential.

We might, for example, discover that one of the biggest irritants for our employees – an irritant being an example of something that has the potential to become a breach when people are under pressure – is a minor rule of limited importance. In this case, we would have two options. We could either ignore the insight provided by RADAR and conclude that there is no point in investing effort for a minor rule. Or, we could recognise that there might be a PR benefit in being seen to change something that we think is insignificant but our employees believe is a big issue.

What Is RADAR?

RADAR uses five radars to highlight where the presence or absence of "tells" highlights where employees are either already in breach or showing signs that they could potentially be in breach of our rules in the future. Understanding where this is occurring or is likely to occur can help us to recognise where our control framework needs strengthening. In other words, where there is a strong likelihood, we will need to deploy behavioural interventions, either adding new ones or removing or enhancing old ones.

The framework increases in complexity, beginning with radars that are more familiar for which data is more likely to be readily available. The later radars are more challenging and designed to encourage you to think creatively about what lessons we might learn from the behaviour of our employees and, therefore, which behavioural interventions might be appropriate.

Each radar within the framework is an adjective that broadly characterises certain types of behaviour that we can see in our employees. They range from the very negative (they're being "rebellious") to the very positive (they're "remarkable"). We'll explore each radar in more detail in the following chapters, but to begin with, here's an overview of the framework. For simplicity, I describe the radars in relation to a single rule, but you can substitute rule for any behavioural intervention of your choice.

Rebellious

The framework begins by looking at the most obvious sign that things aren't working as we want them to. In other words, there is widespread noncompliance with our rule and our employees are being rebellious!

Adaptive

The second radar of the framework encourages us to think about where our employees might be "bending" our rule. If they're bending it today, they could easily break it tomorrow. Equally, bending it might be a form of breaking it that we hadn't considered. Under this radar, we're looking for situations where people aren't noncompliant, but nor are they complying with the rule: they're being adaptive! Perhaps they're complying with the letter and not the spirit of the rule. Alternatively, they might be using a loophole that exists because of a change in circumstances that wasn't foreseen by the person who designed the rule. Or because the rule is poorly drafted. Understanding where and why rules are bent, helps us identify vulnerabilities.

Dissenting

The third radar explores where there is dissent; in other words, a widespread dislike of our rule. There isn't any evidence of widespread noncompliance – or we'd be in "rebellious" territory – but there is some evidence that people don't like the rule. It's potentially an early warning sign that they might seek to circumvent it, either in times of stress or when noncompliance with the rule is a more attractive option than compliance.

Analytical

The fourth radar encourages us to look for instances where our employees are paying particular, possibly undue, attention to our rule. For example, they're asking us lots of questions about it or page impressions shows that it is viewed far more than other rules. If we can find out why people are paying more attention to the rule – in other words, why they're analysing it – we can understand whether this is happening for positive or negative reasons and react accordingly.

Remarkable

The final radar asks us to consider whether the level of compliance or noncompliance we see for our rule is somehow "remarkable". In other words, is what we are seeing in some way unexpected? Perhaps we see very few breaches of the rule when we would statistically expect to see far more, or vice versa. The idea behind the radar is to encourage us to think counter-intuitively. If our rule has produced an unexpected compliance outcome, we should investigate what we can learn from it.

Opposites Attract

Although each radar of the framework points us in a particular direction, in some cases, the opposite can also be worth exploring. For example, "analytical" encourages us to focus on things our employees are paying particular attention to. If our rule generates significantly more questions than others, it may be worth investigating. In Chapter 28, we'll explore why our employees might be asking questions about our rule and what that means from our perspective. But we should also consider "analytical" as a cue to look at things our employees seemingly have zero interest in. So, as well as looking at the rules that generate the *most* questions, we should also consider the rules for which employees seemingly have zero interest; in other words, the ones that create the least number of questions.

We can apply the same principle to "dissenting". While we wouldn't expect our employees to cheerlead for a particular policy or rule, there can often be rules that are actually popular. Perhaps people like the outcome that the rule delivers. Or maybe – remember "H" in HUMANS – the rule is perceived to be helpful. Remember our fictional CEO of BigCo and their dress code? Implementing and policing the policy might have appeared draconian, but its principle could have appealed to many employees. That might happen if, for example, most people already complied with the rule and felt a scruffy minority was letting them down. Knowing that a rule has widespread support can be a helpful blueprint for finding ways to make others seem more palatable.

How to Use RADAR

Like HUMANS, RADAR is not an exhaustive list to be slavishly followed. It's intended to encourage you to think creatively about where you might best apply your newfound behavioural knowledge.

There are two ways you can use the framework. The first involves using it as a tool to review the behavioural effectiveness of a particular rule. I call this the "rules first" approach. For this, you would ask how "rebellious", "analytical", etc., your employees were in response to it. By noting radars where the response to the intervention was extreme – for example, if there was a high degree of "dissenting" behaviour – you could identify the drivers for that and adapt your rule accordingly.

The second is to begin with the radars and look for interventions that are most relevant to that radar (the "framework first" approach). The most obvious example would be to begin by looking at those interventions with most breaches ("rebellious"). Assuming data is available – a subject we'll explore in the next section – we could also look, for example, at which interventions provoke the most "dissenting" behaviour. Looking across the framework also allows us to identify interesting clusters. We may, for example, discover that a particular type of rule poses a behavioural challenge. In this case, we can review that subset, potentially changing them all to make them more effective. Equally, we may find that commonalities, such as how a particular policy is communicated or training is delivered, provide us with an alternative angle.

I have used RADAR with my clients in several ways. One prefers "framework first" and uses it to work through the radars in order, recognising that known breaches (i.e., "rebellious") offer a good starting point with solid data. Another, who also uses "framework first", sees more value in beginning with the more counter-intuitive radars (e.g. "remarkable") as they find it more fruitful and enjoyable to challenge conventional ways of thinking about the issues. A third, let's call them Radar Inc., deploys RADAR "rules first" as part of their annual review of policies asking policy owners to consider how each radar applies to it. Because I think it's the most innovative approach I've come across, I'll highlight any aspects of Radar Inc.'s "rules first" approach that are particularly noteworthy, as we go through the radars.

I am often asked whether it is appropriate to score radars. If that approach works for you, by all means, do so, but remember that, as we saw with HUMANS, there are challenges when we try to quantify qualitative data.

The good news is that there is no right or wrong way to use RADAR. If a particular approach or radar speaks to you, then go with that. If any of them seem irrelevant in your environment or you can't quickly identify things, move on to another.

What Data Do You Have?

A common concern when I introduce RADAR to my clients is that the data that the framework requires might not be readily available. On the one hand, this is an entirely understandable concern. Much of the data that we would ideally have in order to be able to use RADAR might – particularly, in larger organisations where data is often owned and controlled centrally – not be readily available. It may not even exist. Don't be surprised if a request is greeted with "Why on earth would you want to know that?" On the other hand, the fact that we might not be able to get hold of data easily could actually be an advantage.

The Armour Goes Where the Bullet Holes Aren't

In his book *How Not To Be Wrong*, Jordan Ellenberg tells the story of Abraham Wald. He was a mathematician employed by the US military during the Second World War in the Statistical Research Group (SRG). The SRG was a group of mathematicians hired to help solve military problems, one of which was how you could protect aircraft from being shot down. The military had noticed that bullet holes weren't evenly distributed across the aircraft. Far more planes were returning with damage in the fuselage than the engines. They concluded that this meant that the engines needed more armour and wanted Wald to help decide how much they needed. What he said amazed them. As Ellenberg explains, "The armor, said Wald, doesn't go where the bullet holes are. It goes where the bullet holes aren't; on the engines."[2]

His logic was that planes that made it back to base provided data about where the plane could be hit and still return safely. The aircraft that didn't make it back to base were obviously being hit elsewhere. Hence, it was those parts of the plane that needed protecting. They followed his suggestion and the number of planes that returned safely went up.

The logic the military had used is a perfect illustration of something known as Survivorship Bias which relies on WYSIATI. It occurs when we concentrate on people or things that made it past a selection process and overlook those that don't. You can see it in the narrative that successful business people or professional athletes use in their autobiographies to explain the "secret of their success" using a noun like commitment, passion, or dedication.

They're right, of course; being successful does require that and it can be a recipe for success; if, that is, your strategy is a good one and you have the necessary talents. If it isn't or you don't, then single-mindedly pursuing a path is also a recipe for failure. We just don't often hear about the people who failed by following this strategy, because they tend not to get autobiographies published!

Wald looked at the same data set as the military experts but drew an entirely different conclusion. He did this not by thinking about what the data revealed but rather about what the data didn't reveal.

What We Have (May Be) All There Is

As we saw in Chapter 8, when we explored WYSIATI, we are perfectly capable of taking decisions using minimal information. That means we look at readily available information rather than thinking about the data we ideally should or could have. Yet, like Wald, we're often going to find ourselves in a situation where we don't have perfect data. Either because – like the downed planes – that data will never be available to us or because it is not currently available.

Sometimes, what is available to you will be limited by factors beyond your control. If IT systems aren't set up to collect a particular data set, then obtaining it may be impossible, or costly or time-consuming. But it is also worth remembering that "if you don't ask, you don't get". Equally, data that is not available now might be available in future if the people responsible for system updates are aware it's something you have an interest in.

With that in mind, let's explore some data sources we might not ordinarily think of tapping that can provide helpful behavioural insights.

Hidden Data

The first type of data we tend to neglect is what I call "hidden". It's hidden because it is available to us, but we've never seen it or thought to ask for it. The best example is "digital breadcrumbs", the traces we all leave when we do anything online. We're all familiar with how cookies are used to track our digital moves to build a picture of who we are and what we're doing.

For a simple example of digital breadcrumbs relevant to the "analytical" radar, consider a rulebook that has been put online. Anyone responsible for that might not naturally have thought to ask for the capability to monitor how often and for how long our employees look at a particular policy. Yet, if we can do that, we can look for any interesting patterns that emerge from their collective behaviour. As we'll see, if particular policies garner significantly more attention than others, that can tell us something, as can knowing which policies no one ever looks at.

That might not have occurred to us because we're thinking in compliance terms, not media terms. If we consider the handbook not as a set of rules but rather as a form of digital content, then understanding how often that content is accessed becomes an obvious thing for us to do. What we might think of as a "Netflix approach" to compliance, albeit that we've got very different reasons for examining the data.

I'm delighted to report that many of my clients with whom I've discussed this have been surprised to discover that their IT department was quickly able to provide the data; they just had to ask! And those that weren't said they would be able to add the feature on the next update.

Anecdata

In an interview,[3] Amazon founder Jeff Bezos talked about a surprising information source that he uses in his business: anecdotes. On the face of it, people sharing stories about their experiences doesn't seem like a very reliable or representative information source. Indeed, in a digital business like Amazon, wouldn't data be much better? Bezos explained it as follows:

> The thing I have noticed is when the anecdotes and the data disagree, the anecdotes are usually right. There's something wrong with the way you are measuring it.[4]

I call this combination of anecdotes and data "anecdata". From a defensive decision-making perspective, using data is far more justifiable. Yet we know from how we share stories and consume news that the context and reasons why things happen are just as important to us as what has occurred. If we hear something has happened, we also want to know why and what that means. Anecdotes can help us make more sense of what we're seeing or not seeing. Put simply, data can tell us what has happened and the anecdotes why.

While we are often very good at thinking about and collecting data, we often miss the opportunity to capture anecdotes. In part, because the latter is far easier than the former. Data is structured, easy to analyse, and comprehensive; if we request a particular data set, we'll get everything within it. On the other hand, anecdotes are unstructured, harder to diagnose, and highly selective; not every incident will result in an anecdote.

Yet from a behavioural perspective, anecdotes are compelling. Not just because they provide additional colour that might not be obvious from the data but also because they provide insights into what customers think matter. Or, to put it another way, what is salient to them. Amazon customers can, apparently – I haven't tested it myself – email Bezos with their feedback. He claims to look at all of them, though only some are actioned. On the face of it, what he sees in that inbox might not represent the views of the customer base as a whole. But, equally, he knows that some effort is involved in emailing; a customer is only going to write if they feel strongly enough about something. If many customers feel compelled to write about the same thing, he knows it's a big issue.

Anecdotes often appear as part of everyday interactions, but we might ignore them. Taking inspiration from customer service, we know that call centre operatives and other people dealing directly with customers will have insights from their interactions. However, we often don't record them in other contexts. Compliance staff have lots of conversations. Who knows what information we might lose by not doing so?

Undata

If you ever find yourself in New York, pay a visit to the Rare Book division of the New York Public Library and ask to see the Hunt-Lenox Globe. It dates from around 1510 and is one of the earliest-known globes. It is one of only two surviving maps in the world that contains the phrase "HC SVNT DRACONES", in Latin "hic sunt dracones" meaning "here be dragons".

The reference to dragons often appeared in medieval maps to signify uncharted territories. In other words, areas beyond the mapmaker's knowledge. Since these were clearly dangerous, "here be dragons" warned explorers to stay away.

I want to encourage you to do the opposite regarding the data we don't have but know could exist. I call this "undata", and it's surprisingly compelling. On the face of it, non-existent or unavailable data doesn't sound very useful at all. But if we think back to Abraham Wald and the bullet holes on the planes, it was the fact he recognised the significance of the undata that gave him actionable insights.

The trouble with undata is that it is often seen as a sign of failure. For example, many organisations use dashboards showing RAG statuses to monitor progress or risk. RAG is short for "Red", "Amber", and "Green": red is bad news, green is good news, and amber is somewhere in between. It's a perfectly logical way to present information in an easily digestible form. But it can also be highly misleading because it relies on a massive presumption that everything is knowable. Next time you see one, ask where the "Grey" is. What's "Grey"? It's for undata. More specifically, for things we don't know because it's too early to tell or we'll never know.

Knowing where our blind spots are can help us to contextualise the information that we do have. If there are particular rules or policies that we can't monitor – or where we can only monitor with a long delay – then it is essential to recognise that. Otherwise, when we compare behavioural insights for those with rules or policies that we can monitor, we'll get a misleading impression. Remember, as the famous adage puts it, "absence of evidence is not evidence of absence". Just because we don't have any data about something doesn't mean it isn't there.

Data Dynamics

Before we leave the subject of data, I want to highlight a few dynamics that could arise as you try to identify potential data sources. The first is privacy. Since we are using behavioural data, we will obviously need to be mindful of relevant data privacy laws. One of the benefits of looking at collective rather than individual data is that we can use aggregated, anonymised information. This can sometimes permit us to look at things we wouldn't be able to on an individual level. However, we should also remember Rule Number Six; just because we can access data doesn't mean we should. If you're unsure, perhaps think about applying HUMANS to see how your employees might feel about it!

The second thing to consider is the quality and provenance of your data. While I want to encourage you to locate unorthodox data sources to obtain insights into the behaviour of your employees, you should also be mindful that not all data is of similar quality. Remember that for every piece of data you can see, there are probably – made-up number alert! – four you can't. Equally, while data you find from "paths less trodden" can provide incredible insights that you wouldn't find elsewhere, there is also a potential for it to be less reliable than more traditional resources. Though equally, it can be far more reliable. Just because the information has been gathered from a particular source for a long time doesn't necessarily mean that source is more reliable.

The third dynamic is that compliance data is often collected for the sole purpose of answering a single regulatory exam question; something along the lines of "how do you know X is happening or Y is not happening?" Of course, answering those types of question is important. But it can also reduce our ability to look for patterns beyond binary answers to simple questions. We might, for example, know whether staff have completed their mandatory training on time, but have little insights about when they completed it, how long they spent doing so or indeed whether there are any other interesting patterns in terms of how they completed it. The risk we face is that by being given data that answers a specific question, we miss opportunities to ask others.

The most obvious example of the trade-off between "fresh" and "biased" perspectives is the insights we gather from anecdotes. Like eyewitness accounts in journalism, they are compelling. But they also risk being unrepresentative and biased. Sometimes humans offer incredible insights we couldn't get from any other source. But, equally, they can display high degrees of bias, sometimes intentionally and sometimes not. There isn't a simple solution beyond a simple warning to be cautious.

The final thing to remember is not to let the best be the enemy of the good. I like to start from a simple premise: the data we have is better than data we don't have, as long as we understand the data's limitations and give due consideration to the data we don't have in our deliberations. Obviously, don't take data you know to be dirty and make decisions on that basis alone. But equally, if you want to get used to experimenting and trying out new ideas, then having some data sets to hand that you can use to stimulate ideas and formulate hypotheses can be very useful.

Good luck! And if you find any good data sources, do let me know!

Notes

1. For readers unfamiliar with poker, a "tell" is an involuntary change in a player's demeanour that is said to provide a clue as to their perception of their hand. If, for example, a player scratches their nose every time they have what they think is a poor hand, then another player who has identified that can look out for it and react accordingly.

2. Jordan Ellenberg, *How Not To Be Wrong* (New York: Penguin, 2015). You can read an excerpt that tells the story of Wald's work here: https://humanizingrules.link/wald.

3. The quote comes from a fascinating interview with Jeff Bezos at The Bush Center Forum on Leadership from 21 April 2018. You'll find it at the 22-minute mark. https://humanizingrules.link/bezos.

4. ibid

CHAPTER 25
R IS FOR REBELLIOUS

Introduction

The first radar of the framework is "Rebellious", which encourages us to look at situations where our employees are breaking the rules. The radar's simple logic is that if they aren't doing what we want them to, then there's an opportunity to explore why.

On the face of it, this might seem rather obvious. Why on earth, you might rightly think, do we need a radar to tell us that we have an issue when people are breaking our rules?! The answer is that we don't. At least not for the things we know about. However, we need the radar because when it comes to noncompliance, we often only explore a subset of it. Or, to put it another way, what we see may not be all there is!

Rumsfeldian Analysis

I'll explain what I mean with a quote from former US Secretary of State Donald Rumsfeld. It's so famous that mentioning Rumsfeld's name might be a clue for some readers as to where I'm going with this. It's something he said over twenty years ago, in February 2002. Since it appeared to be an attempt to evade answering a question in a press conference, what Rumsfeld said was widely ridiculed at the time. However, outside the political context in which he made it, the comment seems far more insightful:

There are known knowns. These are things we know that we know. There are known unknowns. That is to say, there are things that we know we don't know. But there are also unknown unknowns. There are things we don't know we don't know.

Let's examine how each of these relates to noncompliance.

The most prominent data on noncompliance is *known knowns*, the "things we know that we know". At its simplest, it is data on breaches, where we have some way of knowing whether our employees have or have not complied with a particular rule.

If, for example, there is a requirement to obtain approval before booking corporate travel and an employee books a flight using their corporate credit card, we will – at some point – know whether or not they obtained approval. We know it – or will, at some future point, know it – and we know that we will know it!

However, we often miss opportunities to look further at what that data might tell us.

Crime Data

A technique I have found very powerful when thinking about the information we have on noncompliance is to reframe it. Rather than thinking about it as data on incidents of noncompliance, we can think about it as crime statistics. Not only is that far more exciting, but it also allows us to borrow from another context.

Compare the statement that "last month we saw a 20% increase in breaches of our gifts and entertainment policy" to "last month the number of speeding offences in the city went up by 20%". Of course, they're entirely different things. But context aside, they're communicating similar pieces of information; both are examples of material increases in noncompliance in situations where we know who the perpetrators are.

But there's often a difference between how the police treat crime statistics and how most firms look at compliance data. While the police will look for patterns in their data, businesses tend not to do this with noncompliance. In our speeding example, the police are likely to have considered where most of the speeding occurs, what time of day it happens, what kinds of vehicle are involved and the impact of things like weather conditions. They'll also have considered whether there are any patterns in relation to the way in which people are caught; is it at fixed camera locations or are mobile units more effective? Meanwhile, a typical compliance analysis might only look at who is breaking the rule, not when or even why.

I recognise that the police have greater resources than the average compliance department. And I would not want to suggest that all compliance breaches are akin to crimes. But by asking "what questions would the police ask if this were a crime?" we can identify things we might not otherwise have thought to look at.

Unknowns

Returning to Rumsfeld's framework, the second component is *known unknowns*, the "things we know that we don't know". Most obviously, these are things we can't ever know. For example, assuming we're required by regulation to monitor our employees' work communications, we will only be able to do so if they use official channels. Messages sent via those channels can be monitored, and we know that we can identify breaches of rules; they are *known knowns*. But if an employee goes "off the reservation" and uses an unauthorised channel – an encrypted messaging app like Telegram – then we know that we can't monitor breaches. They are known unknowns.

There is a third category that logically flows from Rumsfeld's analysis but doesn't feature in the quote, which is *unknown knowns*: things that we know but are unaware of. These can be one of two things, depending on whether the lack of knowledge implicit in the "unknown" is inadvertent or intentional. If accidental, it means insights hiding in plain sight that we're just unaware of. For example, a rule for which we have compliance data but have never thought to ask for it. If the unknown aspect is intentional, it means that there are things towards which we choose to display wilful blindness. This could be data we know exists but choose not to look at, or where we do look at it but intentionally misinterpret what it is saying.

Finally, there are the *unknown unknowns*; "the things we don't know that we don't know". Since unknown knowns cover things we intentionally "don't know", this category consists of the information we genuinely don't know and aren't aware that we don't know.

The point of "Rebellious" is, therefore, not just to explore known knowns, though, obviously, they are incredibly valuable. Instead, it is to point us in the direction of the other three categories. By identifying where we have or might have known unknowns, unknown knowns, and unknown unknowns, we will find additional areas to implement behavioural interventions.

My Word Is My Bond

A perfect example of this comes from Financial Services. While the sector is understandably heavily regulated nowadays, this wasn't always the case. The London Stock Exchange, for example, has as its motto the phrase "dictum meum pactum", which is Latin for "my word is my bond". It comes from a time when there were no written contracts, and traders would make verbal agreements to buy and sell stocks. Their word was all that was required to seal a binding contract.

Deploying a similarly trusting logic was an index known as LIBOR. For over 40 years, LIBOR – short for London Interbank Offered Rate – was used to price hundreds of trillions of dollars of financial products. If you took out a loan like a mortgage or a student loan – not just in London, but around the world – then the product's interest rate was likely to have been based on LIBOR. The rate was compiled daily, using an average of estimates submitted by a panel of banks who would provide an educated guess as to how much they thought it would cost them to borrow from other banks. Unlike maths problems at schools, there was no requirement for anyone to share their workings; the submitters just needed to provide the numbers. Even on days when their firm wasn't borrowing money from other banks.

Following the 2008 Global Financial Crisis, regulators began investigations into practices in the financial services industry. In 2012, an investigation into LIBOR discovered widespread manipulation of rates by a number of submitters. In doing so, they made millions for their employers. The firms involved were fined, some submitters went to jail, and at the beginning of 2022, LIBOR was replaced with a far more robust set of alternatives.

With hindsight, it was evident that there was a clear incentive for submitters to manipulate rates. But there were clearly no adequate checks to prevent or monitor whether it was happening. A system that might have worked well for a relatively small number of financial contracts wasn't fit for purpose in the twenty-first century, where there was far more at stake.

I am aware that the vast majority of the readers of this book won't be responsible for regulating benchmark indices. But LIBOR does provide an excellent illustration of how we can easily overlook noncompliance, either because we either don't think to look for it or we don't have data that allows us to look for it.

On the face of it, LIBOR was an excellent example of an unknown from the regulator's perspective. An alternative, more cynical reading is that it was a known unknown that regulators didn't look into until it became necessary because doing so would have required them to act. Whatever the truth, it is clear that no regulator felt they had information that warranted questioning the LIBOR submission process in any detail. Until they did.

WYSIATI Again

One of the simplest ways we can use the Rumsfeld categories is to simply recognise that they exist. In doing so, we can begin to look for *known unknowns*, *unknown knowns*, and *unknown unknowns* and try to turn them into *known knowns*.

Very often, compliance data is skewed towards presenting things that are *known*, rather than helping us to ask questions about the *unknowns*. Like Abraham Wald, we need to think about what we're not being told, as much as about what we are. Recognising that the other categories of data exist can help us to do that. What we see may not be all there is! A simple question of "what *isn't* this telling me?" alongside "what *is* this telling me?" may be all that is required.

The second thing we can do is consider situations when things move between Rumsfeld's categories. While some information on noncompliance is available on a real-time basis – for example, where a breach becomes immediately apparent, and an "alarm" is triggered – other pieces are only available on a delayed basis.

Going back to the example of the fictitious employee who booked travel on his credit card without pre-approval, we won't immediately know they've done it. We'll only find out when the employee tries to claim it or if the company makes direct payment at the point the card company requests.

Until the data arrives, the level of compliance with a particular rule is a *known unknown*; we know that we don't know whether people are compliant. The moment we receive the data, the compliance level becomes *known*. Instead of thinking of the data on the travel approval as always being a *known*, we should think of it as transitioning to that from *known unknown* at a given point in time.

By identifying where this happens – timing is just one obvious example of a trigger point, there are others – we can build up a picture of where we have blind spots and also where we might be able to request additional data that we don't currently have. As we go through the remaining radars, many of the techniques I highlight there can support this.

Practical Application: Radar Inc.

Finally, remember Radar Inc., that client I mentioned who uses RADAR as part of their annual review of policies. When it comes to "Rebellious", they have two different approaches. For the minimal number of policies where there have been widespread breaches, they do the obvious thing and review them in line with what I outlined above.

For other policies, they adopt the idea I highlighted in the introduction of exploring the opposite outcome to the one suggested by the framework. They do this by requiring policy owners to "ethically hack" their policies. In practice, this means identifying weaknesses using the experience gained from any breaches and – this is where it gets fascinating! – asking people in the business to act as ethical hackers.

The ethical hacker's role is to identify weaknesses and explain to the policy owner how they would go about getting around the rules. Either breaking the rules or in the spirit of "Adaptive" – the next radar we'll look at – how they could bend them.

Their ideas for breaking and bending the rules are then formally recorded and, armed with that knowledge, the policy owner updates the policy and associated controls.

CHAPTER 26
A IS FOR ADAPTIVE

Introduction

The second radar of the framework is "Adaptive". It points us to look at situations where employees "adapt" the interpretation of a rule in order to suit their desired outcome. This is necessary where there is a perceived or actual conflict between what they would like to do and what the rules permit them to do. There are two main ways in which this can occur: creative compliance and creative noncompliance.

You've probably heard of the former, but you might not have heard of the latter. In case you're unfamiliar with it, creative compliance[1] is where people comply with the "letter" of a particular rule, but ignore the "spirit" of it. In doing so, they seek to simultaneously benefit from being deemed to be compliant, while also achieving their desired outcome. Creative noncompliance,[2] on the other hand, is where people break the "letter" of a particular rule, but justify doing so by citing compliance with the "spirit" of it.

By way of example, imagine a firm has a rule that prevents the acceptance of gifts worth more than £100 and an employee knows they will be given a case of wine worth £200. A creatively compliant solution would be for them to ask the giver of the gift to split the case into two half cases, each worth £100. In the absence of an anti-avoidance rule specifically preventing the splitting of gifts, this approach would comply with the letter but not the spirit of the rule.

A creatively noncompliant solution would be to accept the gift but seek to justify it by finding a reason why the limit ought not to apply in this situation. The recipient might, for example, argue that although the gift is in their name, they have received it as the team representative, and therefore the £100 limit should be multiplied by the number of team members! Assuming this approach succeeded – unlikely, though I suspect that in certain firms, success might be strongly correlated to the seniority of the gift receiver – it would comply with the spirit but not the letter of the rule.

Successful creative compliance and creative noncompliance differ from the situations covered in "Rebellious", the first radar of the framework, discussed in Chapter 25, because there are no recorded breaches. Either because the creative interpretation of the rules has successfully got through an approval process – and therefore is deemed compliant – or because it hasn't ever been reviewed. Either way, it wouldn't appear as a breach.

Cognitive Dissonance

The reason incidents of creative compliance and creative noncompliance are of interest to us from a behavioural perspective is that they can provide valuable insights. Before we explore those, I want to briefly introduce the concept of cognitive dissonance, which plays an essential part in human decision-making.

In both cases, employees feel the need to indulge in creative solutions because there is a disconnect between what they want to do and what they think or know the rules permit them to do. Mental gymnastics are necessary because of something called cognitive dissonance.

Cognitive dissonance is our mental discomfort when we hold two conflicting beliefs. In the case of the hypothetical wine gift that we explored earlier, the recipients are suffering from cognitive dissonance; on the one hand, they want to be able to justify their decision by reference to the rules. Not just to avoid getting into trouble but also because it feels better to be acting within the rules than outside them. On the other hand, they want to keep the case of wine. They're trying to manage two competing objectives by finding a creative solution.

Rationale

There are three main reasons for looking in more detail at rules that are being bent.

The first is the "slippery slope" argument. If a rule is being bent today, then there's a strong possibility that it might be broken tomorrow. We know people tend to "test the waters" when breaking the rules. From a psychological perspective, it is far easier to break a rule you've already been bending than it is to break one you've always complied with. Remember the idea of repetition suppression that we explored in an earlier chapter? This is an excellent illustration of where that might apply.

The second is that a rule which is already being bent is flawed. This does not necessarily mean that the rule itself is flawed. It could be the training, communication, implementation, or enforcement of the rule that needs to be adjusted. Remember Rule Number Five, "If one person breaks a rule, you've got a people problem; if lots of people break a rule, you've got a rule problem." The fact that lots of people are feeling the need to bend a rule is indicative of the fact that there's a problem with it.

The collective bending is either because the rule is preventing something legitimate from happening, in which case it needs to be bent, meaning it's not fit for purpose. Or, the collective bending indicates that our employees feel it is acceptable to bend it. Perhaps that's what they've always done, or they don't understand or agree with the rationale for the rule. By applying HUMANS to the rule, we can try to establish what the reason is.

The third reason we ought to look at rules being bent is because we have deliberately or inadvertently created an environment where we have tacitly encouraged the bending of a particular rule. Not because we are seeking to encourage rule breaking, but because we recognise that the spirit of the rule is best met through not enforcing hard limits. If that's the case, then it's something we should keep an eye on. A good example of this dynamic is speed limits.

In many countries, the police operate speed tolerance thresholds, levels above the official limits where a small amount of noncompliance is permitted. For example, the UK's tolerance is 10% above the speed limit, plus 2 miles. So, on a road with an 80 miles per hour (mph) limit, the police will only take action against drivers driving at 90 mph. That doesn't mean it's OK to drive at the higher limit. It just means there's a little "buffer zone". But the police still keep an eye on drivers in that buffer zone. You can still be stopped for driving over 80 mph.

Identifying "Adaptive" Behaviour

Before we look at some examples of how we might identify rules that suggest rules are being bent, your regular reminder that we are looking at collective rather than individual behaviour. I mention this here because, in my experience, this is the one radar where people using it are most likely to forget. I think it might be something to do with the fact that looking at rules being bent makes us feel closest to catching someone actually breaking one. Please try to resist that temptation!

With that said, let's explore how we can identify situations where rules are being bent. Spoiler alert: there is no simple answer, but I have three examples illustrating how we might think about going about it.

Know Your Limits

The most obvious place we can look is where there are rules with limits. The benefit of having limits is that they are easy to understand and enforce. As we saw with the example of the case of wine, a numerical limit creates a clear "red line" between compliance and noncompliance.

As we also saw, the downside is that it encourages creativity since it provides a gameable element. If you put a number on something, people can place greater emphasis on the "letter of the law" the number offers than the spirit of the law that underpins it. In other words, the downside of a speed or expense limit is that the primary focus when it comes to compliance is to be within the limit.

However, from a behavioural perspective, this can provide us with some valuable "tells". If, for example, there is an expense limit of $100, then we might want to see whether many people are submitting claims just under the limit. While that doesn't automatically mean they are doing something untoward – after all, there's nothing wrong with claiming something to which you are entitled – but it could indicate that the limit needs review.

Near Misses

We can do something similar for other forms of limit where "near misses" might reveal something interesting. Where there are limits in a rule, there may be an opportunity to look where many people are coming close to breaching it.

For example, if a particular activity is permitted in one jurisdiction but not in another – for instance, if employees need licences to sell a specific product – it might be worth looking at activity near the border area.

If staff from the German office aren't allowed to work in France, but are making lots of business trips to a place on the Franco-German border, then does that make sense, or is it a sign they're actually venturing across the border? On the face of it, they haven't broken any rules, but there's a clear indication the rule may be being bent or even broken.

I've Been Voluntold

As my use of the word "anecdata" illustrates, I'm a big fan of portmanteau words: that's when two words are combined to create a new one. One of my favourites is the word "voluntold", a combination of "volunteered" and "told". It's used to describe the disingenuous practice when someone has been asked to volunteer for something but, in practice, has been told to do it.

This is another example of cognitive dissonance; the person engaging in it wants to be able to pretend people have volunteered, but they also want the benefit of making it mandatory. Voluntelling staff is more common than we might like to admit. It is used to get people to attend presentations, lectures, dinners, training courses, recruitment events, and, most ironically, community affairs volunteering events.

One of the most frequent and probably least egregious things people are voluntold for is completing staff surveys. This can happen almost accidentally, even if the exercise is intended to be voluntary. If response rates across teams are made public or passed to managers, they will likely act to boost their team's participation levels.

While this is understandable, it is also unhelpful from your perspective. Because one of the creative ways we can think about obtaining insights into where people are bending the rules is for us to look at voluntary things as if they were mandatory.

Imagine staff are invited to attend training or participate in a workshop voluntarily, and very few turn up. While that is disappointing from the organiser's perspective, it is also incredibly valuable feedback. We might not know why there is a low turnout, but we have hard data that we can investigate. Perhaps the training is on at the wrong time or has been poorly marketed. Or, perhaps there's something about the content we need to learn from. When people are voluntold to attend, that data is heavily skewed.

However, if voluntelling is unavoidable, then don't worry. There's also potentially something useful there. If they're being voluntold and still not doing it, that's compelling feedback. Because it means they're resisting pressure and still not doing it. So, look for that!

There's some valuable data, whether your employees are genuinely volunteering for things or being voluntold. You just have to work out what's happening to know how to read it. My final tip is if you're ever asking for feedback for voluntary exercises, ask people why they came and add an "I was voluntold" option. Not only will it make people smile, but it might tell you something interesting. Of course, you'll get some mischievous answers, but if you collect enough of them, you might see an interesting pattern!

Finally, the other way we can identify "adaptive" behaviour is when our employees make specific enquiries about the details of rules. We'll cover that when we look at "Analytical", the fourth radar, in Chapter 28.

Notes

1. https://humanizingrules.link/creative

2. Jed Meers, Simon Halliday, and Joe Tomlinson, https://humanizingrules.link/noncreative.

CHAPTER 27
D IS FOR DISSENTING

Introduction

The third radar is "Dissenting". It points us to look for signs of where there is a widespread objection to a rule. There isn't any evidence of widespread noncompliance with the rule – or we'd be in "Rebellious" territory – but there is some evidence that people really don't like it.

We saw with "Adaptive" that rules which are being bent can easily become rules that are broken. The same is true of rules that people hate. If our employees have no respect for, or understanding of the rationale for, a particular rule, then there is potentially a greater likelihood of them not complying with it, particularly in times of stress.

It is also worth noting that a dislike of rules can also come from the outcome the rule produces. Employees might like the idea of a particular rule, until they see the realities of what it actually requires them to do. As we saw in Rule Three when we looked at compliance Theatre, the same applies to outcomes. We can like the idea of airport security keeping us safe, but dislike the additional hassle it causes us. If you're thinking that this is a good example of cognitive dissonance – the idea that we struggle to hold two conflicting beliefs which we explored in "Adaptive" – then you're absolutely right!

Rationale

The idea behind "Dissenting" isn't that we should establish what irritates our employees and just get rid of it. Rather, it is to ensure that if we are irritating them, we are doing so for good reason. There are some situations where we will need to impose rules that are unavoidably irritating. Either because there is no alternative, or because the irritation serves a purpose.

Remember the concept of "Theatre" that we looked at in the context of airport security, where things are deliberately made slower than they need to be? Friction can often result in irritation, if the people who are being slowed down think that the process could and should be run more efficiently. It doesn't matter whether that perception is based on fact or a flawed presumption. I might think that airport security is inefficient and a waste of time, without realising that the fact it feels that way is helping me to notice it exists!

The question we therefore need to ask ourselves is whether the irritation we are inducing is worthwhile. If it is intentional and serves a purpose, then it can be helpful to understand how irritating it is in reality. We might have either underestimated or indeed overestimated the impact of it, in which case, we may want to "dial it up" or "dial it down" to ensure it has the desired effect.

If it is unintended, then we might wish to see what we can do to reduce the impact. In situations where it is unavoidable – for example, a direct result of a regulatory requirement – then we can recognise this and be aware that it potentially poses an increased risk of noncompliance.

Identifying Dissenting Behaviour

How will we know when our employees dislike something? The most obvious way is when they tell us. In some cases, they will do so on an entirely unsolicited basis. While we can't rule out employees expressing an opinion on a particular rule out of sheer curiosity, it is most likely to occur when they have come into contact with the rule.

The most obvious time for this to happen is when they are being trained on it. This is not something we often think to capture when we give training. To the extent feedback is solicited from participants, it tends to focus on the format of the training, rather than the substance. In other words, questions like "Did you find the training useful?" rather than questions like "What do you think about the rule?"

One recommendation I have, therefore, is that you ask people who attend training what they think about the rule they're being trained on. If your training is live, then it can be a very powerful way of stimulating discussion about the rule, since it is not something people expect you to ask. If your training is on demand, then you can ask this as part of any feedback process.

The other reason people might come into contact with a rule is because they have been notified that they are on the wrong side of it; either they've breached it – covered for the purposes of RADAR under "Rebellious" – or are trying to do something which *would* be in breach of it and have been told they can't.

On the face of it, this might not sound like a good idea. After all, asking someone who has been told they can't do something because of a particular rule what they think of that rule is likely to produce a predictable answer. You might, for understandable reasons, be tempted to discount this feedback. But I would caution against that if you do receive any. It is still legitimate feedback, that shapes how they feel about the rule, and potentially your entire framework.

Surveys

If they don't tell us, then perhaps we can ask them. Not just because we might learn something, but also because it sends a signal that we are interested in what they think. The trouble with asking people is that what they give you is likely to be filtered in some way.

They might, for example, be selective about what they tell us. Either telling us what we want to hear, or not being entirely honest. The other reason is summed up in the words of advertising pioneer David Ogilvy: "People don't think how they feel, don't say what they think and don't do what they say." In other words, we're not always reliable witnesses!

I'm not saying don't ask your employees, but recognise that there will be some bias in what they tell you. There will also be some bias in the way we frame the question. We're all familiar with the idea of leading questions, where something is asked in a way that suggests or tends to suggest a particular answer. For example, asking your employees whether they find a certain rule annoying could well encourage them to be more likely to think of it in those terms. Not only does that potentially make your survey data less accurate, but it could also put an idea into their head: "I'd never really thought about it, but now you mention it, that rule is really annoying!"

Ask Disruptively

My preferred approach – and it's by no means perfect – is to ask a more general question, framed in a way that they might not be expecting. The type of question

I like to ask is, "What pisses you off?" or WPYO for short. That might be WPYO about compliance or the rules in general, or it might be WPYO about a specific area of the rules. I use WPYO, partly because it's an unusual formulation, but also because I want to elicit a visceral reaction. I'm less interested in things they find "slightly annoying" and more interested in things they find "incredibly irritating".

The kind of thing that if you were a customer of a business and they asked you to do it, it would be enough to make you question whether you wanted to continue the relationship. This is more powerful than you might think. There are companies whose products or services I no longer use because of a minor customer service issue many years ago. One small thing that PMO, has meant I won't go back to them.

Of course, if you're in the lucky position of genuinely not having anything that fits in that category, then feel free to shift down to "slightly annoying". Though, I would caution you, that I have yet to find an organisation where there isn't something that sits in the WPYO category. It may be worth taking a leaf out of Jeff Bezos' book and asking some more questions!

By the way, my point isn't that you should slavishly follow the WPYO formulation. If you think it's too rude or unprofessional – or not direct enough! – then find your own version. What I'm trying to do is disrupt the normal survey format. Given all the inherent biases in surveys, I want to ensure that we have the best possible chance of getting "unsterilised" insights of where our rules might pose an issue.

Finally, remember that you can also ask the opposite question. Perhaps we can follow the far politer lead of decluttering guru, Marie Kondo. In her book *The Life-Changing Magic of Tidying Up*,[1] Kondo asks people to use this simple question to determine whether or not they should keep a particular item or get rid of it: "Does it spark joy?" Finding out which, if any, of our rules employees really like – or let's be realistic, "quite like" – can also provide some interesting insights. There may, for example, be features of the things that "spark joy" which you can replicate elsewhere.

Feedback Matters

Do be aware that if you ask people what they think of something, there is an implicit expectation that you will use that information in some way. After all, no one likes being asked for their opinion, only to have it ignored. This is why many companies do "you said, we did" type presentations to showcase how they have used insights gleaned from employee surveys. Usually these are heavily curated and ignore suggestions that are either too difficult to implement or deemed to be undesirable.

My recommendation is that if you are going to ask employees what they think about the rules, that you're also transparent about what you're not going to do and, importantly, explain why. A "you said, we didn't" approach. Not only is it far more honest, but it also shows people that you have at least considered what they told you.

That doesn't just matter in the context of asking them about the rules. It can also send a signal for how you might treat whistleblower or "speak up" reports. If your employees think you're not listening when you've specifically asked them a question, then they might conclude that you're even less likely to do so when they come with something you haven't asked them for.

Actions Speak Louder Than Words

An alternative to asking your employees, or having them tell you, is to observe their behaviour. Actions, as they say, speak louder than words. While we need to be wary of misinterpreting what we observe, there is often a lot we can learn from how our employees react to our rules.

The first is that they put off doing whatever the rule requires. It's a natural human trait to avoid doing things we know or think are likely to be unpleasant. You only have to look at how many people submit their tax returns at the last minute or after the deadline to see this in action. In the UK, for example, in 2022, 630,000 people – that's 6% of taxpayers – filed in the final 24 hours before the deadline, while a further 2.3m (19%) missed it entirely.[2]

We can see the same thing happening in the work environment. If employees think a piece of mandatory training is likely to be tedious – either because they've had previous experience of it or because they've been given that impression by others – then they may well wait until close to the deadline before completing it. Or, they might not do it at all, in the hope that the problem goes away.

However, do remember that might not be the only reason. If you've sent it at a time when the people required to attend are under a lot of pressure, the delay may well be because they have other things to do. The content might be fine, but the timing is not. In that case, bad timing could well be a tipping point that turns something that would ordinarily seem reasonable, into something that feels entirely unreasonable.

The second is that they seek to comply with the rule in a very basic way. While this is not as obvious a measure as the timing of when they do something, it can sometimes be possible to find proxies for low quality compliance. If, for example, there is a requirement to submit free text – as part, for example, of an approval process – it may be possible to use length of response as a proxy for engagement with the policy. Of course, the amount of text is not necessarily a proxy for the quality of the entry, but if there are similar processes, it may be possible to benchmark against those.

Notes

1. Marie Kondo, *The Life-Changing Magic of Tidying Up* (London: Vermilion, 2014).

2. https://humanizingrules.link/tax.

CHAPTER 28
A IS ALSO
FOR ANALYTICAL

Introduction

The fourth radar of the framework is "Analytical". It encourages us to look for instances where our employees pay a lot of attention to our rule. For example, they're asking us lots of questions about it, or the page on which the rule appears on the intranet receives significantly more traffic than similar pages.

If we can find out why people are paying more attention to the rule – in other words, why they're analysing it – we can understand whether this is happening for positive or negative reasons and react accordingly.

Rationale

The reasons we want to explore why people are looking in detail at our rule are most simply illustrated by a familiar plot you'll recognise from the movies. In *The Great Humanizing Rules Robbery*, an imaginary film I've just invented, the main protagonists are a gang who are – the clue was in the title! – planning a robbery. This requires them to scope out a secure facility, which conveniently happens also to run visitor tours.

The gang disguise themselves as tourists and join a visitor tour. What *we* know, but the tour guide does not, is that she is about to guide two very different types of visitors. There are genuine tourists who will ask questions because they're interested and fake ones who will do so to find weaknesses in the facility's security that they can later exploit.

We experience broadly similar dynamics when our employees pay attention to our rules. As the fictional movie plot illustrates, there are two main reasons they are likely to do this.

Genuine Interest

The first reason people will pay attention to rules is that they are genuinely interested in understanding them. On the face of it, this is a positive since they are clearly motivated to try to do the right thing. However, as we will see, there are situations where this is good news – primarily where making enquiries is precisely how we *need* them to behave – but others may be more illustrative of a problem.

Fence Testing

The second reason people spend time researching rules is that they're looking for loopholes. If the effect of a rule is particularly obstructive from the employee's perspective, then there's an incentive to look for ways around it. Equally, if the rule is "gameable" – for example, it contains lots of technical details in a rapidly changing environment – it is potentially more loophole friendly.

Clearly, "genuine interest" and "fence testing" are not mutually exclusive. It is possible that someone enquires out of genuine interest and realises that gaming the rules or noncompliance is preferable. This can happen when they become aware that compliance is more challenging than they had imagined or when something they intended to do clearly breaches the rules. Alternatively, it may be that someone who is testing the fences realises that compliance is actually easier than noncompliance.

FAQ Logic

To understand when an enquiry might be a positive sign and when it might be a negative one, we can think about the dynamics of the rule in question. There will be specific topics or rules where we might naturally expect or indeed want our employees to ask questions. There will be others where an enquiry seems unusual.

My point isn't that we should treat all enquiries of a particular kind as suspicious and questions of another kind as innocent. Just because someone is making an enquiry that could be suspicious doesn't mean they are actually doing something wrong. It is perfectly possible for people to forget things or to be curious for a good reason. Equally, people up to no good can look entirely innocent.

This is one of the reasons I like to focus on collective rather than individual behaviour. If many people are looking at something, there's a collective message. Of course, the downside of collective data is that Fred might look at something in a very different way from why Francesca is doing so. But it's a start, and if we look at collective behaviour, we may find some interesting patterns. It's also worth remembering that the purpose of looking at where employees are being analytical isn't so that we can catch them out. Instead, it can help us to identify where there is a pattern of behaviour that should prompt us to investigate why.

I refer to this as FAQ Logic from the Frequently Asked Questions we see on websites. FAQs are things that website owners have identified are common questions – either things they initially expected users of the site to ask or things they have discovered that they frequently ask. They then look to answer them; either by redesigning the website, so the questions don't arise or by answering them. We can adopt a similar approach when employees ask questions about rules. One of the ways is to think about whether an enquiry is expected or unexpected.

Expected or Unexpected?

If, for example, a particular rule is only relevant in limited circumstances – for example, when someone travels – then it may be entirely reasonable for someone who infrequently travels to need to remind themselves of the rule. But we might be surprised by a frequent traveller doing the same thing.

The same applies to processes or rules that employees must follow at different frequencies. Someone who only has to do something once a year, who refreshes their memory before doing it, is more expected than someone who does something regularly and feels the need to do it.

Equally, there is a difference between rules or procedures that might apply at entirely unpredictable moments as opposed to predictable ones. We explored a few examples of these in Chapter 4, when we looked at three different examples of training we might want to provide for employees. By way of reminder, they were as follows:

- *Awareness*: where we need employees to know the "telltale signs" of a dynamic and then either take a specific course of action (e.g. not to click on an email link) or get help.

- *Understanding*: where we need employees to have a basic understanding of a situation so that they are well-informed enough to be able to make the right choice from a series of potential responses (e.g. knowing whether to fight or flee from a fire).

- *Autonomy*: where we need employees to be able to use their judgement to respond to a fluidly evolving situation (e.g. administering first aid).

A simple analysis might conclude that employees investigating anything covered by these three types of training is entirely predictable and, therefore, a good thing. Awareness, for example, is intentionally designed to make them aware of something, not to give them any level of expertise in the subject. Hence, someone recognising they only have limited knowledge might be a good thing. However, it is worth considering what level of enquiry might be appropriate.

Someone undertaking detailed research into a topic where Awareness is all we need them to have could indicate that they are trying to solve problems without getting appropriate help. If, on the other hand, they are simply revising their basic understanding, then that is arguably far more positive. Equally, someone requiring Understanding diving into technical details may also be trying to bite off more than they can chew. Conversely, if someone should have Autonomy or a greater understanding of an area looking at fundamental concepts, it could be indicative of a surprising lack of understanding.

Alternatively, we may be dealing with something I call the "Hypothetical Actual".

The Hypothetical Actual

An option which didn't feature in my fictional movie but, in my experience, is prevalent in real life is the "Hypothetical Actual". It works as follows. Someone enquires about a particular rule and wants to run a hypothetical scenario past you. My working heuristic in these situations is always assuming that nothing is hypothetical.

This is particularly true if the level of detail is greater than one might expect from a hypothetical situation. The chances are that whatever they are asking about has already happened, and they're either seeking reassurance that what they've done is within the rules or are looking for a potential loophole.

The other feature of these enquiries is that they are often presented as an "asking for a friend" type request, usually on behalf of a staff member whose name they don't want to reveal because "it doesn't matter at this stage". If you come across this, be wary, but also recognise that they should be having the conversation rather than not.

Identifying "Analytical" Behaviour

Identifying when our employees are being analytical can sometimes be challenging because there is a broad range of ways in which they might do so. Some of these will provide digital breadcrumbs, and others won't. To help you think about where you might find this information, here are three examples of ways they might choose to obtain further information about a rule, each with commentary on some of the dynamics.

The first is through unofficial channels, where they undertake "research" by, for example, asking a colleague. On the one hand, this may be the easiest way for them to obtain information. On the other hand, it can also be because they are trying to avoid official channels. They might be looking for an unofficial interpretation of the rules; in other words, the same reason the lady I mentioned in Chapter 14 asked for advice on whether she needed to put a label on her luggage. In that case, they may be seeking an answer along the lines of "the rule says X, but no one actually does that". Equally, they might want an initial response to enable them to frame their "official" question more effectively.

The "research" method is hard for us to detect. After all, we're unlikely to get employees telling us that other people have asked them about a particular rule. Though it may be something, you can obtain anecdotal insights about. It is also worth noting that "research" can also pose the greatest risk, as the colleague they ask may not necessarily have a good knowledge of the rule in question.

The second is via self-service channels such as reading the staff handbook, reviewing online training, or other online resources. This can provide easily gatherable data since it is a breadcrumb-rich environment. What is worth noting – if your system allows – isn't just what they are looking at, but how they ask questions. There may be helpful information in the way that questions are formulated and the substance of what is being asked.

In his book, *Everybody Lies*,[1] Seth Stephens-Davidowitz outlines how we are much more likely to be honest with a search engine than we are with another human being. While discussing the risks posed to individual privacy, the dynamic of being more transparent is still relevant in an employment context. The reason for our over-disclosure of our digital versus human interfaces is that we might choose to "sugar-coat" our question if we're asking a person so that we're not embarrassed or revealing too much about the reasons for our question. But when it comes to asking a search engine or online portal for help, we get better results by being direct.

The final category is that they go directly to the experts, for example, by contacting their Compliance Officer. This can provide the richest source of information, as there will be more context to the enquiry. Training those who receive the questions to pay attention to what they are asked and the context in which they are asked can provide some handy insights.

Good News or Bad News?

As ever with RADAR, don't forget that we can look at the opposite dynamic. If there's a policy or rule that no one ever looks at online or asks questions about, that could also be worth investigating. Whether you choose to do so will depend on the nature of the rule. If it's something obscure, then perhaps the fact that no one is focussing on it is not a matter of concern.

But if a rule is more likely to result in questions, we might want to ask why no one is doing so. It may well be that everyone is aware of, understands and is compliant with the rule and the reason no one is looking at it is because there is no need for them to do so. At the opposite end of the spectrum, perhaps no one is aware the rule exists, and therefore it does not occur to anyone to look at it. Alternatively, maybe they know it exists but are not interested in discovering more about it.

Whether the reason for the lack of interest is a good thing or a bad thing will depend on the rule in question. The only way you'll know is to look at the policy and investigate further.

Teaching Rule-Breaking

I want to share something that illustrates an alternative way of thinking about "Analytical" employees. On the face of it, one might consider that an appropriate way of dealing with analytical enquiries designed to identify how to break the rules is to shut them down. That would have been my gut instinct as well.

Until I read about Timpsons, a UK-based family-owned company that provides services like shoe repairs, key cutting, dry cleaning, engraving, and assisted photo ID. There's nothing unusual in that business model, but what differentiates Timpsons from other companies is that they actively set out to employ ex-offenders to give them a second chance. Around 10 per cent of their workforce is made up of people who have criminal convictions.

In a *Times* newspaper column headlined, "I always show staff how to put their fingers in the till",[1] the CEO, James Timpson, explained:

> To reduce theft levels, we tell our colleagues the best ways to steal from us. It sounds counterintuitive, but if everyone understands that we know how it works, they're less likely to do it in the first place. If you know a speed camera is around the corner, you slow down. Every six months, we publish in our newsletter an updated list of reasons colleagues have been dismissed and what they have done. The top five are always the same, but there's often a wheeze we haven't spotted before.

What I like about this is that he's given real thought to what his employees might be thinking – in other words, what might make them "Analytical" in future – and hit it head on. They don't need to find out for themselves if he's told them. And they know that he knows.

Practical Application: Radar Inc.

When it comes to "Analytical", my client Radar Inc. provides policy owners with information about how many questions were asked about their policy and details of the critical topics that were asked. The idea isn't for them to need to amend the policy to deal with each question but rather to see if there are common themes that might warrant amending the policy.

They are also asked to find someone to "mystery shop" the policy and report back. The purpose of the mystery shopper is to do two things. The first is to establish how easy it is – or isn't – to obtain information on the policy. It's one thing having a policy, but is it easy to find if you don't know what the policy is called? The answers then feed into the policy review.

The key to this radar is to think the unthinkable. While we don't hire employees on the presumption that they will test our rules, it is important to recognise that some will, for good and for bad reasons. This radar encourages us to prepare for that fact.

Notes

1. Seth Stephens-Davidowitz, *Everybody Lies* (London: Bloomsbury, 2018).

2. https://humanizingrules.link/timpson.

CHAPTER 29
R IS ALSO
FOR REMARKABLE

Introduction

The fifth and final radar in the framework is "Remarkable". Like the other radars, it takes insights from our employees' behaviour. However, unlike the other radars, its focus is not on understanding their behaviour. Rather, it is there to help us to better understand how we are designing and implementing our framework of rules.

The radar uses something we would probably otherwise not think to look at; rules where we find unexpected levels of noncompliance; either rules where noncompliance rates are unexpectedly high or unexpectedly low.

While rules with high levels of noncompliance in *absolute* terms will already be identified under "Rebellious", "Remarkable" identifies rules that have *unexpectedly* low (or high) levels of noncompliance. In other words, levels of noncompliance that we weren't predicting.

Rationale

There are two main reasons for looking at rules with "remarkable" levels of noncompliance:

The first is to assess the design effectiveness of our rules. By comparing how we thought a particular rule would "perform" with its actual "performance", we can assess how effectively our rules have been designed.

The second is that it can help to sharpen our behavioural antennae. If we mis-judge our employees' propensity to comply with a particular rule – by either over- or underestimating it – then understanding why can provide valuable insights.

Two Unspoken Truths

This radar builds on ideas we have explored throughout the book. The key one is that rules can and should be treated as attempts to influence human decision-making. On the face of it, the word "attempt" seems inappropriate. After all, rules are mandatory and backed by an authority, so we tend to expect people to follow them. But we also know that not all rules are followed all of the time; if they were, there would be no need for this book!

For these purposes, I think it is helpful to use an (admittedly loose) analogy of rules being akin to advertisements. Both are forms of behavioural interven-tion. Just as advertisements are attempts to influence people to buy products or services, rules are attempts to influence people to behave in a particular man-ner. However, unlike rule writers, advertisers are more likely to recognise the experimental nature of their work. Before launching an advertising campaign, advertisers will have some idea of what impact they expect the advertisement to have. Not least because they'll need that to justify the expenditure of producing and running it. Then, once the campaign has gone live, they can compare the actual performance with what they were expecting. Companies don't launch advertising campaigns without some idea about how effective they'll be.

Like advertising campaigns, rules also have a cost associated with them; it's just not as obvious. For every rule, there will be an effort required of employees to comply with it and an effort in implementing compliance initiatives to maintain and enforce it.

To do this effectively requires us to acknowledge two generally unspoken truths about compliance. They're things that marketers understand intuitively when it comes to advertising, but we tend not to think about in a compliance context.

The first unspoken truth is what we saw in Chapter 22; when lots of people fail to comply with a particular rule, it's a rule problem, not a people problem. When we "craft" rules – as when marketers create advertisements – they aren't always perfect. So, when employees fail *en masse* to comply with our rules, it isn't entirely their fault!

The second unspoken truth is that even when we "craft" our rules perfectly – at least from a theoretical perspective – they don't always work the way we expect them to. In Chapter 12, we explored the concept of "a fine is a fee", where rules intended to deter a behaviour encouraged it. Just as adverts don't always achieve their expected result – even with the best market research in the world – the same will also be true of rules.

Note that word "expected". When I say that the rule hasn't achieved its expected result, I don't mean that the rule didn't achieve 100% compliance, which, as we know from Rule Number Two, is not always feasible or desirable. I mean that it didn't fulfil a realistic expectation of what it would deliver.

What Is Realistic?

So, if 100% isn't always realistic, what is? Obviously, the answer will depend not just on the rule, but also on how it is perceived by employees. To repeat the mantra that has appeared throughout this book, we need to think not about how we would like our employees to perceive it, but how they are likely to perceive it.

By way of example, imagine that we introduce a rule that every member of staff will be required to take an extra paid day of holiday a quarter. In most cases, this rule is likely to be positively received and we should expect very high levels of compliance with it. It is unlikely to be 100%, but in the absence of, say, pressure from line managers not to take it, it should be very high.

Then imagine we introduce a rule that bans employees from bringing personal mobile devices into the workplace. That is likely to be far less popular and it would be reasonable to expect far lower rates of compliance.

Of course, the specific circumstances of the workplace in question will be highly relevant. People working for employers where there is huge pressure to meet sales targets might not want to take an additional day's holiday. Staff working in highly sensitive workplaces may well easily comply with the rule banning mobile devices. But it will, on some level, be possible to have a view as to how likely employees are to comply with a particular rule.

The idea behind the radar is that we formulate a hypothesis and then compare what happens with what we expected to happen. If compliance levels are unexpectedly high or unexpectedly low, then we should investigate why. Say rates are far higher than expected; is that because people are actually complying or because we are measuring the wrong thing? Or perhaps they have found a loophole. Or did we misjudge the likelihood of compliance? Whatever the explanation, we can learn something useful by exploring.

Expectation Management

In order for this radar to work, we will need to have an idea of the likely level of compliance. There is no hard and fast rule about how to do this, but here are three suggestions for ways of thinking about it:

The first is on a "rough-and-ready" basis by looking at known compliance rates and asking policy and rule owners to identify anything that has surprised them. While this might yield results, it offers the obvious incentive for them only to identify policies where compliance levels are higher than expected and ignore those that are lower. It also requires them to be honest about what level they expected.

The second way – which requires some effort and planning – is by asking policy- or rule-owners to estimate the difficulty of complying with their policy or rule when it is initially launched or as part of a review process. This can be done using a simple scale – say, one to five – and then using that as the basis for comparison.

Obviously these first two measures are highly subjective. But it is worth remembering that we're not looking for scientific analysis; we're just trying to get a rough idea, for the purposes of encouraging those creating the rules to think about "compliability".

We also need to create an environment where the exercise isn't about being "right" or "wrong", but instead is about learning. What we want to avoid is incentivising those responsible for writing the rules, to "game" what we're asking them to do! That would be ironic!

The third and more objective method is to use peer group analysis and look at how one rule performs relative to its peer rules. That peer group might be rules covering a similar topic – for example, all rules on anti-bribery and corruption – or it might be rules of an equivalent length, or which apply in similar circumstances. For example, we might compare all rules related to foreign travel since they will all apply in the same context.

In doing this, we can identify where our expectations of how the rules would be complied with haven't matched up to reality. We can then identify why and see what lessons we can learn. Not just about our employees, but also about our own behavioural antennae.

CHAPTER 30
CONCLUSION

Lessons from a Sexologist

In July 2020, I was scrolling through my Twitter feed looking for new ideas when I came across a tweet that grabbed my attention.[1] The first line read as follows:

> If you want to know how we get people to comply with wearing face masks, ask a sexologist.

Obviously, the word "sexologist" made the post incredibly salient. I didn't know any sexologists, so I wanted to learn what advice they might be able to give. But I also loved that this was someone drawing compliance lessons from one field and applying them in another. If a sexologist thought there were some parallels, I wanted to know more. The second line of the tweet read:

> It's not our first rodeo when it comes to convincing people they should wear a barrier for protection from a deadly virus.

Suddenly it became clear where the thread was going; insights from stopping the spread of HIV could provide lessons on how to stop the spread of COVID. Genius! I read on.

> You can't shame, guilt or judge people into compliance. Does not work.

Wow! This *was* interesting. You don't have to be a sexologist to see sense in that statement. And then:

> Help people to learn the communication skills needed to talk to others they encounter who don't want to wear one.

Music to my ears! It was pure "think about how people are likely to behave rather than how we'd like them to behave!" The thread continued with eight other equally insightful and behaviourally brilliant tweets. So, I did exactly what you'd expect. I got in touch with the person who'd written the tweets, Jill McDevitt, and invited her onto my Human Risk podcast to tell me more. She said yes, and we spent an hour exploring it together.[2]

Borrow Good Ideas

It's the perfect illustration of the main lesson I want to leave you with at the end of the book. When faced with compliance challenges, we tend to look at what we've done before or what other people in our field are doing. Yet, as Jill has illustrated, sometimes we can find inspiration in a completely unrelated area.

We can often find solutions in the most unusual places by simply reframing our compliance problems as behavioural challenges. Lots of the examples I've provided in this book of how BeSci can help influence human decision-making are in a marketing context. That's a discipline where they're looking to maximise sales of a product or service, so they make sure that they test all of their ideas thoroughly to get the best possible answer before they release their intervention into the wild.

In a compliance context, we often don't have that luxury. Not only are we not set up to do lots of testing, but we don't have the time. Surprisingly, this can actually be an advantage, because it means we can move more quickly. Unlike marketing, we're not seeking to maximise outcomes; if we can make our population more likely to do something by making small changes, that's great. If changing the wording in an email, for example, can increase compliance rates from 60% to 70%, that's a positive. There might have been an option to get that number up to 77%, but we'd have had to do many experiments to find that out. I contend that if we can make things better, then we should. A small win is better than no win.

Compliance in the Wild

As we end our journey, I hope the examples I've shared inspire you to think differently about how we can influence our employees. One of the most exciting things is looking all around you for ideas. Everywhere you look, you can find examples of compliance requirements imposed on us; some successfully, some not. That might be when you board a bus, go to a supermarket, cross the road, enter an office building, or log onto a website. All have the potential to inspire solutions to compliance challenges. Or, indeed, provide reminders of what not to do.

As a final example, here's a longer case study involving a client of mine, who took inspiration from "compliance in the wild" to a whole new level. I think she's come up with a really innovative solution. As with all the ideas in the book, my aim is not for you to slavishly copy them. Though feel free to borrow any aspects that you find appealing. Instead, the idea is to highlight where we came up with our ideas and how we transformed them into practical solutions.

How Frequent Flyer Programmes, Doctors Appointments, and Customer Service Emails Helped Humanize Rules

I'll call my client Jenny. She's Head of Compliance at a large multinational, and she was having problems getting people to complete their mandatory training on time. In common with the rest of their industry, the company needs their employees to complete a certain number of training modules each year.

We began by scoping out the problem they were facing. Jenny explained that their approach to this was as follows:

> We send out the email inviting our staff to take the training and tell them they've got 30 days to do it. Then, if they haven't completed it, every five days, we send them a reminder. In the final few days, we send them a reminder every 24 hours. If people haven't done it 48 hours before the deadline, we email their line manager.

Jenny explained that a significant number of people either did it in the final 24 hours before the deadline or missed it entirely. That, she explained, led to the idea of emailing their line manager so that they could also put pressure on the individual. This entire process had created additional admin for the training team and meant that many employees needed to be disciplined because they'd missed the deadline. While the line manager email had improved things, it hadn't worked as well as expected.

When we discussed the problem – using HUMANS as a basis for analysis – we realised there were a few challenges from a behavioural perspective. Six things immediately struck us as problematic, based on our anecdotal data.

1. Email

The first thing we looked at was the email. When Jenny had first described it to me, she'd used the word "invite", but I thought that was just her way of describing it.

It turned out that they were sending out "invitations" to mandatory training! It wasn't the first time I'd come across that formulation. As I explained to Jenny, if the training is mandatory, inviting people to attend is disingenuous; it's either an invitation, which the recipient can refuse, or a mandatory requirement, which they can't. It cannot be both. They were potentially irritating the recipients before they'd even read the email!

Then there was the content of the email. The training was described in very technical terms and referenced the rule it covered. Not only did it not sound very interesting, but there was nothing in the description that made it sound at all relevant to the average employee. That, I figured, probably wasn't helping matters.

2. Timing

Then we looked at the timing. I asked Jenny how they decided when to send the email out. The answer was that they used automated scheduling software, which, it transpired, could easily mean that the system would send out emails on Friday afternoons. Not great, as it meant they were effectively sending emails at a point that the software thought was convenient, not necessarily at a convenient time for the people taking it. Since it wasn't evident to recipients that the timing was being scheduled by software – remember WYSIATI! – the email could easily lead recipients to believe that Jenny's team had deliberately chosen the timing. That was fine if it landed at an appropriate time but terrible if it didn't.

3. Deadline

We then discussed the deadline. On the one hand, 30 days sounds like a reasonable time to do a training course. But 30 days doesn't give anyone a particular sense of urgency either. It could engender a propensity to "kick the can down the road", particularly if the subject was something that didn't interest them. On the flip side, not all 30-day periods are the same. A 30-day period that begins on 24th December, just before people go off on their Christmas holidays, is not the same as 30 days that start on 24th January. Jenny confirmed that the system had no blocks on it, meaning it was perfectly possible emails could go out offering "anti-social" 30-day periods.

4. Reminder Emails

Then there were the reminder emails. While they were ostensibly designed to be helpful, they contained an implicit presumption that someone who completes the training as soon as they receive the email "invitation" is somehow more compliant than someone who does it in the final hour before the deadline. Both are equally compliant, yet someone adopting the latter strategy receives unsolicited emails cajoling them. The line manager's emails before the deadline also seemed quite an aggressive policy. Thirty days, after all, means 30 days!

5. Messenger

We also looked at "the messenger". In other words, the mailbox from which the email came. While it shouldn't matter who sends an email, we know it does. The email came from an anonymous training mailbox. Might that, I wondered, have an impact?

6. Target Audience

Finally, the target audience. We looked at who was being sent the training. It turned out that for administrative reasons – aka the convenience of those organising the training – the training team had decided that every employee would take the training, even those for whom it wasn't relevant. Better, it was thought, safe than sorry.

The Solution

Having done a workshop to explore these areas, here's how Jenny and her team went about solving the problem.

The first thing they did was to rewrite the email to be more customer-friendly. Jenny and her colleagues looked at letters and emails they'd received in their personal lives from organisations that needed them to do things and looked for customer-friendly wording they either liked or didn't like. The former would help inspire, the latter were things to avoid.

They reviewed utility company requests for meter readings, letters from doctors' surgeries asking them to make medical appointments, and even one from a tax authority requesting payment. They found customer-friendly wording they liked, and while they didn't copy it verbatim, they took inspiration from things they found engaging. It's the very opposite of WPYO. They removed the word "invitation", changed the email's wording to explain what the training would cover – not from a theoretical perspective, but a practical "what's in it for me" angle from the recipient's perspective – and made an effort to make it sound more salient.

Then came my absolute favourite part of this whole exercise. The new email informing recipients of the need to do the training offered them a simple deal. They could have 30 days to do the training, but they could have one day's credit for every two days they did so ahead of the deadline. With certain restrictions, the email recipient could then use that credit to give them more time to complete a future training course within the following 12 months.

Two things inspired this. The first was that many loyalty schemes – airlines, for example – have huge unused points balances that people have accrued but never get around to using. Perhaps people would respond similarly when it came to training credits. Why not bank them just in case they ever needed them? Plus, people like collecting things, so why not give them something to collect? By ensuring the credits expired, we would avoid people being able to roll training over into perpetuity! The best part of this idea is that the credits cost absolutely nothing. You're creating something the employees might value out of thin air.

The second inspiration was a text message Jenny had received from her doctor inviting her to make an appointment at a time of her choosing. This inspired the concept of working with employees who would need to do the training to find a time that suited them. The invitation nudged them to make this during the following 21 days to ensure there was some slack but gave them the entire 30 days if needed. Even if they received the email at an inopportune time, they would be "invited" – for once, a good use of the term! – to pick a slot in their diary they felt they would be free to do the training. It would then schedule a diary appointment for them at their chosen time.

The system then only sent the person doing the training a single reminder email the day before the slot they had chosen. It would only send chaser emails if the recipient failed to do the training at the time they had committed to do it. If people cancelled the training, they'd be sent a reminder and a link to rebook.

They also decided that the email invite would be sent from someone the recipient would know. Since we already knew they could identify the recipient's line manager, the invitation was sent out from them by, but not from, the automated system. The line manager chaser emails were then only sent if the individual missed the deadline.

The last change was probably the most significant. My client limited the training to those for whom it was felt to be genuinely necessary, documenting the rationale behind their choice in case a regulator asked. And they added one fur-ther option. Employees who received it could apply for a dispensation if they could provide a good reason why it might not be relevant to them. Interestingly, very few did.

There are three lessons to learn from this. The first is that we can take inspiration from anywhere. As you'll have noted, the ideas came from contexts that were nothing to do with compliance.

The second is that while, in an ideal world, we'd have run experiments to test each change, that's not always possible in the real world. When faced with a compli-ance challenge, you often don't have the luxury of testing things before imple-menting them.

The third lesson is to know what you're trying to achieve with particular interven-tions and monitor them to ensure they're doing what you intend. Since we were removing impediments and things that were unpopular with the old approach, it was unlikely – though not impossible – that the overall package of changes would make things worse. Fortunately, it made them much better.

And, Finally

I will finish the book with the answers to two of the questions people commonly ask me when I talk about humanizing rules.

"So, How Would You Have Prevented the Oscars Envelope Error?"

My suggestion would be to remove as many distractions as possible, ignore the context, and look at what the task involves. Partners don't usually do administra-tive tasks like handing out envelopes. So, let them stick to the red-carpet stuff and stay well away from envelope management.

Ideally, you'd find a junior staff member, but the responsibility might overawe them, so I'd go for a mid-ranking person. They'll remember what it's like to do administrative tasks and bring some experience. The final criterion is you want someone who detests the movies, so regardless of what happens, their focus will be on the job.

"Since You Don't Like the Word 'Compliance', What Would You Call the Function Instead?"

My initial reaction is "anything but Compliance"! Though there isn't really an obvious alternative. "Adherence", a term used by the medical profession to describe the act of following a prescribed course of action, is one alternative. As is using words like "Ethics" or "Integrity". But I think a smarter way to approach this is to recognise that there is one huge benefit to the "Compliance" brand. It sets really low expectations that anything you do to humanize the function will seem much more impressive!

Thank you for reading the book. Do get in touch to share how you've used the ideas in it. You'll find me on LinkedIn and Twitter if you search for "Human Risk".

Notes

1. https://humanizingrules.link/jill.

2. https://humanizingrules.link/sexologist.

ACKNOWLEDGEMENTS

My former colleagues at the Bank of England and UBS for inspiring the thinking that led to this book. Particularly the ones who were supportive of my attempts to challenge the status quo.

Jim Oates for being a great boss and providing the springboard for Human Risk to grow into what it has become.

Dr Colin Lawrence and John Sutherland for their continuing support and interest in what I'm doing.

The many academics who have inspired me to learn more in this field, including Professors Yuval Feldman, Benjamin Van Rooij, and J.S. Nelson.

All the behavioural scientists who have been so kind with their time, particularly Rory Sutherland, Jez Groom, Gerald Ashley, and Paul Craven.

My fellow explorers in the intersect between Behavioural Science and Compliance fields, notably Ricardo Pellafone, Roger Miles, Ruth Steinholtz, Chris Hodges, Richard Bistrong, and Tom Hardin for encouragement, challenge, and providing different perspectives.

Nic Frank for the countless "walk & talk" sessions during lockdown that helped me develop my thinking.

Mark Heywood for being a critical friend and a provider of wit, wine, and wisdom.

All the fabulous guests on the Human Risk podcast for being generous with their time and knowledge.

ACKNOWLEDGEMENTS

My parents, David and Inge Hunt, for actively encouraging me to be curious, challenging, and giving me the head start in life that led to me being able to write this book.

Finally, Esther for supporting, inspiring and putting up with me; generally and specifically during the many, many hours I spent writing this book. Thank you for being there on the journey with me.

ABOUT THE AUTHOR

Christian Hunt is the founder of Human Risk, a consulting and training firm specialising in bringing behavioural science to ethics and compliance.

Christian's practical experience of deploying behavioural science to solve real-world problems began in an informal sense when he conducted several unsupervised, unscientific experiments as a small child. These have continued to influence his work. Not least because he still bears the scars. More formally, he was a managing director and head of behavioural science at UBS, a role specially created for him following his pioneering deployment of it within compliance and risk. Christian joined the firm in compliance & operational risk control, leading the function globally for UBS Asset Management and regionally for UBS Europe, the Middle East & Africa (excluding Switzerland).

Before joining UBS, he was Chief Operating Officer of the Prudential Regulation Authority, a subsidiary of the Bank of England responsible for regulating financial services. He'd never intended to become a regulator; but, when, in 2011, the Financial Services Authority came looking for a new Head of Department to help change the shape of regulation after the 2008 financial crisis, he jumped at the chance.

He has also worked in a family office and as an investment banker. Christian began his career at Arthur Andersen in regulatory and financial consulting. His most memorable project was matching dormant accounts in Swiss banks with lists of Holocaust victims.

He is a Member of the Global Association of Applied Behavioural Scientists, a Fellow of the ICAEW, and a Fellow of the Royal Society of Arts. He also holds an MA from the University of Oxford.

ABOUT THE AUTHOR

Christian speaks and writes regularly about BeSci and human risk. He also hosts and produces the Human Risk podcast. You can find him on Twitter at @human-riskltd. He divides his time between Munich and London, travelling between the two cities by train.

INDEX